The RV Cookbook

Carol Meredith

Published by

1 Main Street Burnstown, Ontario, Canada K0J 1G0
Telephone 1-800-465-6072 or FAX (613) 432-7184

ISBN 1-896182-33-X
Printed and Bound in Canada

Cover Illustration by Honz Petersen
Interior Design by Leanne Enright

Canadian Cataloguing in Publication Data

Meredith, Carol
A taste for travel: the R.V. cookbook

ISBN 1-896182-33-X

1. Cookery. 2. Outdoor cookery. 3. Recreational vehicle living. I. Title.

TX840.M6M37 1995 641.5′75 C96-900691-5

First Printing 1996

Dedicated to my recipe tester,
intrepid adventurer,
partner in life,
fixer of anything that breaks
and special friend,
Alex

Acknowledgments

Thanks are due to the many people who helped with this project. I am grateful to all the RVers we met on the road who responded to my announcement that "I'm writing a cookbook," with enthusiasm, and recipes. Many of them are named in the book; thanks to them and also to the others who didn't stop long enough for me to write down their names. I am very grateful to my son Mike and his friend Alissa for their ideas and support on our special recipe-testing trip from Vancouver to Santa Fe. Heartfelt thanks to my electronic community, the members of the Litforum and the RVforum on Compuserve, especially to Janet McConnaughey for help with the title, and to Bonnie Schutzmann, Fay Zachary, Robert Lee Whitmire, Karen Pershing, and Eldon Garlock for reading and commenting on some of the stories. I thank my publisher, Tim Gordon, and the staff at General Store Publishing, for their interest, advice, and encouragement.

Table of Contents

Beginning
the Journey

RV kitchens are small, and ours is one of the smallest. Our motor home has only minimal cupboard space, but it is equipped with a good refrigerator, a freezer compartment, and a four-burner stove with a tiny oven. There is minimal space to store pots and pans, dishes, and canned goods. The spice rack that my son Mike gave me for Christmas last year is tied into the corner on the kitchen counter. I don't have a microwave, although most of the more modern RVs come equipped with one. I don't have a blender, a food processor, a mixmaster, or even a toaster. I didn't know I could live without those things, but I learned how! I store my frying pan, a square cake pan, a rectangular pan, a muffin tin, and a cookie sheet in the oven, since they won't fit in the cupboard. I keep two pots and a couple of aluminum foil bread pans under the sink. The cookie sheet doubles as a broiler pan, and we make toast on it under the broiler as well. My kettle hangs on a hook behind the stove when we're travelling. That's my batterie de cuisine for now.

We added a small portable barbecue to our equipment, and it hooks onto the propane tank that runs our stove, refrigerator, and water heater. What a luxury! You'll see from the recipes that we use it a lot. Sitting outside under the awning to cook supper is great, and it keeps the motor home cool in places like southern Arizona, where it's hot even in April.

I didn't intend to become a full-time RVer. My partner Alex and I bought a motor home (a 1978 Itasca, 23 feet long) to get us from Quebec to the west coast of Canada, with stops along the way, to visit children and grandchildren. We thought it would be a bit more comfortable than camping, and less expensive than staying at bed and breakfasts, that's all. Little did we know! By the time we reached the west coast, we had discovered a new lifestyle that we thoroughly enjoyed. Nine months later, I still prefer a house with wheels.

I also didn't think that cooking in an RV would be very interesting. We'd camped before, and cooked a bit on a little camp burner, but making breakfast in the rain is no fun at all when you've only got a tent, so we ate out a lot. In the RV I discovered that it is actually fun to make supper together after a day's driving, and that breakfasts are easy to do. Even lunches pose no problemand are both faster and cheaper than stopping at a restaurant, ordering, waiting, eating, and paying. The best part is shopping for food all around the country. When we're busy, we shop at a supermarket every two or three days. Other times, we ferret out the local produce markets or buy fish and seafood right by the ocean.

I keep a journal of our travels, and some of our experiences are worth sharing. So, although this book is predominately a cookbook, a lot of stories insisted on being included. All of the recipe testing was done as we travelled, from southern Quebec to the shores of the Atlantic Ocean, then west to the Pacific, and most recently from Vancouver Island down the coast to California, across to New Mexico, and then back to British Columbia. I'm sure all these recipes will work in your camper, trailer, fifth wheel or motor home, and expect that my stories, although different from yours, will remind you of your own on-the-road experiences, either real or imaginary.

There are three different situations in which we find ourselves as RVers. Some of us prefer one to the others. Alex and I have sampled all three. When we first started out, we spent a lot of time visiting friends and relatives, parking in their driveways. As far as cooking goes, this type of RVing means making our own breakfast most of the time, and then sharing meals with our hosts for the rest of the day. Sometimes we invite them out to the driveway for supper, or cook for them in their house kitchen for a change. It's the easiest way to visit that I know, once we convince them that we really are self-sufficient, and just want to be neighbours for the time that we're there. I particularly recommend it for visiting grown children with grandchildren. Ashley and Sean, Alex's grandchildren, are fascinated by Grampa's house on wheels when we visit their home in Calgary. Sean and his friend, who are both four, spent a long happy time figuring out how the latch on our bathroom door worked. Ashley comes out after breakfast to visit and invites us in. We are out of their way during the family's morning routine, and they are out of ours too! Ashley and Sean enjoy helping me test the cookie recipes in particular, and all the other members of the family vote for their favourites.

By far the most popular way of living the RV lifestyle is to stay in parks with full hookups. This means that there's a place to attach the RV to electricity, water and sewer systems, and sometimes cable TV and a phone as well. We lived this way for three months in Crofton, BC on Vancouver Island, as well as for shorter stays here and there along the way. In northern California, for instance, we stayed overnight in a place with cable so that Alissa, one of our passengers on that trip, could satisfy her longing to see the Academy Awards. In this situation, cooking is much like it is in a normal kitchen, with the only restriction being space. My counter top is eighteen inches wide, plus I have a board twelve inches wide that fits on top of one-half of my double sink. Alex usually chops vegetables sitting down at the dinette. Some of the full hookup parks we visited in Arizona and California have lots of activities going on, including potluck suppers. The folks in these places are very friendly, so I do my best to produce an interesting dish to share.

We also spent two weeks on partial hookups (water and electric but no sewer connections) in a special place called the Jojoba Hills SKP Resort in southern California. Along with the recipes I learned there, you'll find stories about this enthusiastic group of people and the RV park that they are building cooperatively.

Our favourite way of living in our motor home, though, is boondocking. This simply means stopping somewhere and staying until it's time to move on. We carry enough fresh water to last about four days if we are careful, and have space in our gray and black water tanks for three days' worth of waste water and sewage. The batteries supply us with power, though not enough to run the air conditioner. Many of the newer RVs, particularly the larger motor homes, can carry enough water, etc. to last for a week or more, and people get very good at conservation! We now have solar panels on the roof to recharge our batteries, so there's no need to use the engine or a noisy generator. This is a wonderful way to enjoy the natural beauty of our continent. It is fascinating to have new landscapes, trees, flowers, birds, and even animals in our front yard every few days! We have boondocked on mountains, beside the ocean, and just driven off the highway into the desert for the night. Several boondocking stories are in among the recipes here, and some of the recipes are designed to use very little water or propane gas.

There's a special section of recipes and suggestions for salt-free, low-fat and sugar-free diets, as well as recipes in the other parts of the book which also adhere to these restrictions. More and more of us are conscious of the need to watch our intake of salt, fat and sugar. The folks living in RV's are often retired, or wishing they were, and having found this lifestyle are determined to keep healthy as long as possible to enjoy it!

The recipes I use are mostly very simple, and take little time to prepare. Most RVers I talk to on the road agree with me that the best recipes are easy to make, attractive looking, delicious, and healthy. So those are the aims that I've kept in mind in selecting this collection. I've included variations with some of them, and of course you should feel free to try your own. There are only two things I really look for in a cookbook. One is that it be fun to read, and stimulate my imagination with some ideas I hadn't thought of before. The other is that it have proven recipes that are easy to try. So that's the kind of cookbook this one is meant to be. I hope it will enhance your enjoyment of an important part of the RV lifestyle.

Breakfast

Our first mornings on the road were spent in the driveway of our friend Mary's farm. We woke to the sound of a crowing rooster and the mooing of cows in the pasture across the road. When we discovered the leak in the black water tank, Alex borrowed tools from Mary's son Fred to fix it, while I retreated hastily to the house bathroom. Blocks of wood to stick under the wheels to level us up were available in abundance. The first morning we ate breakfast in the farmhouse kitchen, but after that we enjoyed the luxury of taking our time, watching the morning bustle of feeding the pigs, collecting eggs from the henhouse, and doing barn chores from the motor home window. Since then we've had some mornings when it's important to get up and on the road early, but for the most part we savour a slow beginning to the day, and take the time to cook and eat a leisurely breakfast.

Pancakes or Fluffy Flapjacks

I used to consider making pancakes a big performance, much more difficult than other breakfasts, but really it takes no more time to make them than to do an omelette. A friend in northern Vermont taught me to use yogurt or cottage cheese in them, for extra protein and a nicer texture. I like the yogurt version best. I call these pancakes, but I've been corrected several times by folks who insist they're really flapjacks. It doesn't matter what you call them. They're delicious!

2	**eggs**	**2**
1 tbsp	**melted butter or margarine**	**15 mL**
1/2 cup	**plain yogurt**	**125 mL**
3/4 cup	**milk**	**175 mL**
1 cup	**flour**	**250 mL**
1/2 tsp	**baking soda**	**2 mL**
1/2 tsp	**baking powder**	**2 mL**
1/4 tsp	**salt**	**1 mL**
1 tsp	**sugar**	**5 mL**
1/4 tsp	**cinnamon**	**1 mL**
	butter or margarine for cooking and spreading	
	maple syrup or jam	

Melt the butter or margarine in the frying pan while you beat the eggs well in a mixing bowl with a whisk or a fork. Leave the frying pan off the heat until the batter is ready. Add the melted butter or margarine, yogurt, and milk to the eggs and beat well. In a measuring cup combine the flour and other dry ingredients. Then add the dry mixture to the liquid and beat it up some. It will still be a bit lumpy, which is fine. Pour 1/4 cup (50 mL) of batter per pancake on the hot greased frying pan. Form two or three pancakes at a time, depending on the size of your pan. I make them small, as they're easier to turn. When there are bubbles all over the surface, it's time to turn the pancake over. Cook slightly less time on the second side, until the underside turns golden brown, then serve and repeat the process. Serves two pancake lovers, or three with smaller appetites.

These pancakes are very light, and are best eaten straight out of the pan. I cook while the others eat, and then take the last batch for myself. If you must keep them hot, put them in the oven at 200° F (95° C), but they may go limp!

VARIATIONS:

Apple Pancakes: Add 1 washed, cored, and chopped apple to the batter after combining the liquid and dry ingredients. You may also add 1/2 tsp (2 mL) of nutmeg if you like it, for an extra bit of flavour.

Lemon Pancakes: Add 2 tsp (10 mL) of lemon juice to the egg mixture and the grated rind of 1 lemon to the dry.

Berry Pancakes: Add 1 cup (250 mL) of fresh or defrosted frozen berries to the batter. Blueberries, strawberries, raspberries, blackberries, or any combination are great.

Raisin Pancakes: Add 3/4 cup (175 mL) raisins to the batter.

In the Provincial Park at Kemptville Ontario

There's something totally decadent about being in a park campsite in the motor home. What luxury! We have all the enjoyment of a campfire, a picnic table, and walks beside the Rideau River, while at the same time enjoying a hot shower in our own bathroom, and a gas stove on which to cook breakfast! Not to mention a cellular phone, computers, our own bed . . . it's a great way to live!

Next door is a family, mother large in a blue sweat suit, father even larger in a voluminous T-shirt and sweat pants, a two or three-year-old daughter, and a baby in a stroller. Oh, I forgot the dog, a white dog with black splotches here and there, tied to the leg of the picnic table and getting his chain wound round and round the baby's stroller. Father left in the car about nine thirty last night, and showed up again at eight this morning. I guess he must be afraid of the dark, or perhaps he's working a night shift somewhere? They have a little Boler trailer, plus a red tent, a playpen, the stroller, lawn chairs, the chain for tying up the dog, and the other paraphernalia of baby parenthood.

On the other side, there is a family in a tent trailer, whose friends also reappeared this morning. The family, mother, father, and at least three little girls, all slept in the trailer, while a second family came back in the Dodge van this morning. The parents have been moving bedding out of the tent trailer into the trunk of their car for about an hour now. The fire is burning, and the portable barbecue with propane tank stands on the picnic table.

It makes our set-up seem totally decadent. We arrived last night, put two boards under the left-side wheels to level it up, plugged in the electricity, and got the lawn chairs down off the roof. Then I went in search of firewood. I found a little concession store where they sold me a load for three dollars. The young man asked me where we were staying, so I told him. He said, "Oh yeah, that must be the big motor home I just saw pulling in. I'll take it down for you." So while I walked off to explore the river bank, he delivered the wood to our campsite! Alex was slightly annoyed at the interruption, as he was already busy working on the latest refinement to his gas mileage spreadsheet on the computer.

Now, in order to leave here, we need to put the computers away, lock the fridge door, and, oh yes, not forget to switch the fridge from 110 power to gas. We'll unplug the power, put the lawn chairs back up in the storage pod on the roof, and the blocks from under the wheels back in their compartment. Lock that up and we're ready to go. No great packing, no tent to strike.

Alex already made up the bed, while I started chopping the vegetables for our breakfast omelette. We've had the hot water on, for showers and dish-washing, and turned it off again. I haven't swept the floor yet, but it only takes two minutes. And that's all there is to it.

Campground Omelette for Two

1	**onion**	**1**
1/2	**green pepper**	**1/2**
6	**mushrooms**	**6**
2 tbsp	**minced fresh parsley**	**25 mL**
	or	
1 tsp	**dried parsley flakes**	**5 mL**
1 tbsp	**butter or margarine**	**15 mL**
5	**eggs**	**5**
1/8 tsp	**salt**	**1/2 mL**
1/4 tsp	**ground pepper**	**1 mL**
1 cup	**grated cheddar cheese**	**250 mL**

Chop the onions, green peppers, mushrooms, and parsley. Melt the butter or margarine in a large pan and sauté the vegetables in it. Beat the eggs with the salt and pepper in a bowl until frothy. Set the vegetables aside in a bowl. Pour the eggs into the pan and sprinkle the grated cheese on top. Cook over medium heat until the egg mixture is set. Spread the vegetables over one-half of the omelette. Cut the omelette in half and fold the half with no vegetables over the half that has them. Cut it in half again and serve.

Broiled Ham and Cheese Open-Faced Sandwiches

This is one of our favourite breakfasts, but lots of people like it better for lunch. We eat bread and butter pickles with it, which my son thinks is a very strange thing to have first thing in the morning! I just smile and tell him he doesn't have to eat it if he doesn't want to. I used to make this with bacon instead of ham, before I became aware of the amount of fat I was consuming. It's good for breakfast, lunch, or a hot snack after walking in the rain.

3	**thin slices honey ham or Black Forest ham**	**3**
4	**slices of bread**	**4**
1/4 lb	**sharp cheddar cheese, sliced thinly**	**100 g**

Cut the ham slices in quarters and put them on a pan under the broiler. I use a cookie sheet, as I've yet to find a proper broiler pan that fits in an RV oven without placing the food too close to the flames. Let the ham cook a little bit while you arrange slices of cheese on top of the bread slices. Then bring the pan out of the oven. Top each cheese slice with a piece of ham, cooked side down. Lay the open-faced sandwiches on the pan and put the pan back under the broiler for a few minutes, until the cheese is melted, the ham is a bit curly, and the edges of the bread are brown. Serves 2 for breakfast, with pickles.

French Toast

This is one of those old familiars that you've probably been making all your life. It's a great thing to do with slightly dried-out bread! I added a twist to it, since I didn't like the idea of using a lot of sugar and salt. Of course, Alex still pours maple syrup all over it, and there's usually both sugar and salt in the bread, but at least there's none in the recipe! Here are the quantities for 2 people. For more hungry folks, just add an egg per person and some more spices.

3	**eggs**	**3**
3 tbsp	**milk**	**45 mL**
1/4 tsp	**nutmeg**	**1 mL**
1/2 tsp	**cinnamon**	**2 mL**
1/2 tsp	**grated lemon or orange rind (optional)**	**2 mL**
1 tbsp	**butter or margarine**	**15 mL**
4	**slices of bread**	**4**

Beat the eggs and milk in a bowl with a whisk. Add the spices and beat some more. Melt the butter or margarine in a frying pan. Dip each slice of bread in the egg mixture, coating both sides well, then fry it until lightly brown on both sides. Instead of the usual maple syrup, try serving it with unsweetened applesauce or marmalade on top.

Snacks &
Light Meals

I confess that I really don't believe in the idea that you have to eat three times a day, at eight, noon, and six. The other day we got up at five, since we wanted to check back with our friend the mechanic before taking the motor home on a two hundred and fifty-mile drive from Vancouver Island across the mountains to a rally in the Okanagan. So we ate breakfast at seven. By the time we drove off the ferry at ten thirty, my stomach began to rumble. It was too early for lunch but I wanted to eat something. It got me thinking about snacks. On the ferry we'd watched as the girl in the cafeteria put up the specials for their next run across the Georgia Strait. Aha, baked potatoes with a variety of toppings! I resolved to experiment. Alex ate salt and vinegar chips as we cruised toward Hope, then fell asleep while I drove up the Coquihalla Highway toward Merritt. Later we traded ideas for potato toppings, or stuffings, and the recipes in this section grew out of that conversation. There was snow on the side of the road at the summit of Highway 97c– this at the end of May–but when we got to Peachland it was hot. Not just warm, but truly hot. Shorts, T-shirt and sandals hot. Cold snacks came to mind, including the celery boats that I used to make for my children when they were little and hungry before dinner. So here's the collection of light bits and pieces, all much more nutritious than those salt and vinegar potato chips!

Baked Potatoes with Toppings

Bake the potatoes, one per person, or half if they look bigger than your appetite, either in the oven or, if you have one, in the microwave. Don't forget to pierce them, as they make a terrible mess if they explode. When they're cooked, cut a cross in the top and open them up, using oven mitts to protect your fingers. Spoon the topping on and serve!

Traditional Topping (amounts for one potato)

1/4 cup	**sour cream**	**60 mL**
1 tbsp	**chopped fresh chives**	**15 mL**

Spoon the sour cream over the potato and sprinkle with chives.

VARIATIONS:

One: For a no-fat alternative, just substitute nonfat yogurt for the sour cream.

Two: In place of the chives, try chopped fresh parsley, chopped fresh dill, chopped fresh basil, or a combination of any of them, with or without the chives.

Three: Fry two rashers of bacon until crunchy, then crumble them and sprinkle the bits on top of the chives and/or herbs.

Four: You may also add, in combination or by themselves, chopped walnuts, chopped olives, chopped celery, and green peppers, etc.

Five: You can make this a fix-your-own by putting out chopped herbs, crumbled bacon, olives, walnuts, celery, green pepper, sweet red pepper, chopped mushrooms, or anything else that suits your fancy and letting each person build his or her own topping.

Garlic Topping

1	**clove garlic, peeled, mashed and minced, or squeezed through a garlic press**	**1**
1/4 cup	**sour cream**	**50 mL**

Mix the garlic into the sour cream and then spoon over the potato. If the garlic is too strong this way, just mince it without mashing, or use 1/2 tsp (2 mL) of dried garlic instead.

Variation: Add chopped fresh herbs such as parsley, dill, or basil along with the garlic. You may mix them in or sprinkle them on top. You can add crumbled bacon to this also, if you like it.

Cheese Melt Topping

1/4 cup	**grated cheese, cheddar, mozzarella, or a combination of your favourites**	**50 mL**

Cover the top of the potato with the grated cheese and put it on a pan under the broiler or on a plate in the microwave until the cheese melts.

He-Man Chili Potato

1	**baked potato**	**1**
1/4 cup	**chili, heated**	**60 mL**

Cut the potato in half lengthwise on a plate and smother with chili.

Variation: If you're really hungry, you can then top it with grated cheese, as in the previous recipe. The cheese should melt on its own, but, if it doesn't, put it under the broiler or in the microwave for a short time.

Celery Boats

At rallies of Good Sam chapters and whenever there are two or more Escapee members in one place, four o'clock is Happy Hour. Bring your chair, your drink, and a snack to share. Mostly, the snacks are chips and dips, or veggies and dips. Here is an alternative, which I also make whenever I'm playing grandmother or aunt to young visitors.

4	**big stalks of celery**	**4**
	peanut butter	

Wash and dry the celery, trim off the tops and the bottom ends, and cut them into 2 inch (5 cm) lengths. Spread peanut butter into the boats and arrange them on a plate. Why dry the celery? If you don't, the peanut butter won't stick!

Variation: Use cream cheese, plain or with flavourings, instead of the peanut butter.

Garlic Toast

Great with spaghetti, other pasta dishes, lobster tails or just by itself while watching TV.

1/2 cup	**butter or margarine**	**125 mL**
2	**large cloves of garlic**	**2**
1/4 tsp	**dried parsley flakes**	**1 mL**
6	**thick slices of French bread**	**6**

Soften the butter or margarine. Peel the garlic cloves, mash them with the blade of a knife and mince fine, or put them through a garlic press. Add the garlic and the parsley to the butter or margarine and mix well. Spread the garlic butter on the bread slices. Put them on a cookie sheet under the broiler to toast. If you have more garlic butter than you need (it depends on the size of the bread slices), put it in a covered container in the refrigerator until the next time.

Sandwiches

Alex and I just love sandwiches for lunch, which makes it very easy! Usually we put cold meats, cheese, lettuce, tomatoes, mayonnaise, mustard, pickles, and anything else we want, out on the table, and each make our own. Complications only arise when we have guests.

Recently we picked up our friend Bonnie at the ferry terminal in Nanaimo and set out for Long Beach on the west side of Vancouver Island for the weekend. Part way there, the engine started to hiccup and all three of us felt nervous. We had passed Port Alberni and the ominous sign that says No services for 85 km. So the question was, Do we go on, or do we turn back? It was lunch time, so we stopped for sandwiches. One of the nice things about breaking down in a motorhome is that we have everything we need with us: food, a bathroom, our own bed, the cellular phone for calling for help. Alex took the sandwich makings out of the refrigerator, and Bonnie slid into the corner of the dinette bench. She looked at what he had put out, and asked, "Do you have any peanut butter?" She was a bit shocked when I said no. "No peanut butter? How do you manage without peanut butter?" Finally she settled for cheese, onion, dill pickles, and lettuce, but stated firmly that the next time she travels with us she'll bring her own peanut butter. After lunch we decided to keep going, and the motor home made it to Tofino, at the far end of the road, with no mechanic on duty! The beach was beautiful, fourteen miles of glorious sand and rocks and surf, so we limped noisily into the campground for the night. We climbed down to the beach, and strolled about, watching the gulls fly above the surf as the sky turned sunset colours. On Sunday the terrible noise magically stopped, and the motor home made it back to Nanaimo in time for Bonnie to catch the six o'clock ferry. Later that week we found a wonderful mechanic who worked with Alex to fix the problem, which is another story. (His wife taught me the trick to cooking fresh crab, so I put it in the fish section.) What I really remember about that weekend, though, is Bonnie's recipe for her favourite sandwich filling.

Bonnie's Sandwich

2	**slices of bread, preferably whole grain**	**2**
	peanut butter	
2	**slices of mild onion**	**2**
1	**thick slice of cheddar cheese**	**1**
	lettuce	
	mayonnaise	

Spread peanut butter on one slice of bread, mayonnaise on the other. Put the onion on the peanut butter, the lettuce and cheese on the mayonnaise. Then put the sandwich together.

Alex's Favourite Sandwich

2	**slices of bread, preferably white**	**2**
	butter or margarine	
	mayonnaise	
4	**slices of smoked meat**	**4**
2	**slices of sharp cheddar cheese**	**2**
2	**slices of tomato**	**2**
	lettuce	

Butter one slice of bread, and spread mayonnaise on the other. Put the meat, cheese, tomato, and lettuce on the buttered bread, and top with the slice which has mayonnaise as well. This sandwich needs to be eaten sitting down with two hands! Once I made one for him while Alex was driving, but it proved impossible to eat with one hand on the wheel.

Carol's Favourite Sandwich

2	**slices of bread, cracked wheat**	**2**
	mayonnaise	
2	**slices of Black Forest ham**	**2**
	Dijon mustard	
1	**large dill pickle, sliced**	**1**
	lettuce	

Spread mayonnaise on both slices of bread. Put the ham on one slice, then spread Dijon mustard over it thinly. Top with the dill pickles, lettuce, and the second slice of bread.

Ploughman's Sandwich - North American style

medium salsa
thickly sliced French style white bread
thickly sliced old cheddar cheese
lettuce

Spread the salsa on both slices of bread, and make a sandwich with cheese and lettuce.

Practising for the Dragon Boat Race

One afternoon in May we went down to the beach in Chemainus, looking for a quiet place to spend a few hours. It was lovely and peaceful for a while. Then a whole group of vehicles arrived, two with handmade boats on top. It was one of the local Indian tribes, ready for a training session in the dragon boats. The whole tribe came, not just the kids who were practising. The little ones ran to the swings and the young men stood about examining each others' paddles. Some of the men and women strolled down to sit on the rocks by the shore, while another group supervised the launching of the boats. They used one big dragon boat and three single canoes.

The enthusiasm was contagious, so I abandoned my attempt to write and went out with Alex to talk with them. There were two teams practising, one of kids under thirteen, and the other of young men. The adults told us proudly that they all came down every afternoon to cheer them along. The younger ones went off and did a two-mile run, while three of the women used the single canoes. As the young team returned, everyone gathered on the shore and yelled Finish it! to encourage them. The man with the stopwatch announced proudly that they'd taken twenty seconds off their time. Then the young men took over the boat and went off on an even longer paddle. One of the men told us they race every weekend all summer. A mother remarked that they also run every day and have to watch their diets to stay in shape. The younger children played in the water while the adults visited and laughed on shore. When the practice was over, they loaded the boats back on top of the pickups and piled back into their cars. The beach was quiet once more.

Chopped Egg Salad Sandwich Filling

2	**hard boiled eggs**	**2**
1	**green onion, chopped small**	**1**
1	**small stalk celery, diced**	**1**
1 tbsp	**mayonnaise**	**15 mL**
1 tbsp	**fresh parsley, minced**	**15 mL**
	or	
1 tsp	**dried parsley flakes**	**5 mL**
	salt and pepper	

Peel and chop the eggs in a bowl. Add onion, celery, mayonnaise, parsley, salt and pepper. This mixture may be used with cheese, cold meat, tomato, and/or lettuce on your favourite bread.

For a different taste, add 1 tsp (5 mL) or more of curry powder to the parsley.

Soups

I used to love making soups from scratch when I lived in a house with a real kitchen. Whenever I roasted a chicken, turkey, goose, or duck, I'd boil the leftover carcass in my stock pot, with the skin and a bit of vinegar. After straining the stock and refrigerating it, I'd skim off the fat and pour the stock into small containers for the freezer. I made beef stock, veal stock, turkey stock, duck stock. It was so easy to make wonderful soups from that! I froze the stock in small quantities, usually in old one or two-litre plastic ice cream containers, and pulled it out of the freezer when needed.

In my RV kitchen, I don't roast poultry. Birds of roasting size simply won't fit in my oven. I can't even boil a whole chicken that's big enough to bother with, as I only have small pots. I really don't like boiled chicken, anyway. So for a long time, I made do with canned soups. The instant bouillon cubes are too loaded with salt for my taste. I thought, and thought, trying to come up with a way of making stock. Then I realized that chicken wings might work. So one night I broiled up two pounds of chicken wings for dinner. After we finished eating them, with Alex complaining that he didn't really like chicken wings, and it was an awful lot of work, and messy to eat them, even though they tasted great, I made stock with the bones. I'm happy to report that it worked just fine, and I came up with a pint of good-quality chicken stock. Not enough to freeze, but certainly enough for a good soup for the two of us.

Chicken Stock

	bones, skin and any leftover meat from 2 lbs. (1 kg.) of chicken wings	
	water to cover	
1 tbsp	**vinegar**	**15 mL**

Put the bones, etc. in a pot. Add enough water to cover them and the vinegar. I use whatever vinegar I have on hand. The vinegar trick was given to me by my old friend, Naomi, who used to make her stock with chicken feet and has never travelled in an RV, as far as I know. Boil it hard for 20 minutes or so, then let it cool. Strain it into a container and refrigerate it overnight. The next morning skim off the congealed fat. If you want to, freeze it in the same container, or pour it into smaller ones. If it has solidified in the refrigerator, heat it again to pour. It will keep for one week just in the refrigerator, or a month or two in the freezer.

After I wrote this section, I realized that I could make beef stock too. All I had to do was find a butcher who would sell me some marrow bones. I remind myself not to buy too many! The method is the same as for the chicken stock.

Vegetable Soup - From Scratch! - No Added Fat or Salt

2 cups	**chicken stock**	**500 mL**
2	**cloves of garlic, optional**	**2**
1	**chopped onion**	**1**
1	**chopped carrot**	**1**
2	**stalks celery, sliced**	**2**
6	**medium mushrooms, sliced**	**6**
3 tbsp	**chopped fresh parsley**	**45 mL**
	or	
1 tbsp	**dried parsley**	**15 mL**
1/2 tsp	**pepper**	**2 mL**

Refrigerate the chicken stock overnight, and skim off the fat. Then put it to heat in the soup pot. Peel the garlic cloves and cut them in half. This gives a lovely mild garlic touch to the soup. If you want a more pungent garlic flavour, mince it, mash it with the side of your knife, or put it through a garlic press. When the stock is boiling, add all the vegetables. Once it boils again, turn it down to simmer. Add the parsley and the pepper. Allow the soup to simmer until the vegetables are tender. The length of time this takes depends on how big the pieces are. Serve with bread or scones and cheese.

Jojoba Hills

This recipe is from Sandy Arnold, one of the enthusiastic volunteers at the Jojoba Hills SKP Resort in Aguanga, California. We stayed two weeks there, helping out, and I collected several great recipes. Alex was the hero of the day when he got their plotter to work with the computer, so that they would be able to produce copies of the resort plans on demand. What an enthusiastic bunch of people! The resort is nearing completion after several years' work by a changing population of co-op members and other volunteers. Marty Gillespie, a retired hairdresser, pumped out all the black and gray water tanks and did welding on the huge culvert pipes. His wife Eleanor was in charge of the landscaping crew when we were there. Ken, our next-door neighbour, and his wife, work on the cement crew. Sandy, who gave me this recipe, zooms around on her personal electric vehicle, lending a hand and a smile wherever it is needed. She says this recipe makes enough for two meals for her husband and herself, and it's even better the second time it's heated.

Sandy's Bean Soup

1 can (14 oz)	**white beans**	**398 mL**
1 can (14 oz)	**stewed tomatoes**	**398 mL**
1/2 cup	**instant brown rice**	**125 mL**
1/2 can (6 oz)	**Mexican corn**	**170 mL**
	or	
1/2 cup (4 oz)	**frozen Mexican corn**	**125 mL**
1/4 lb	**extra lean ground beef**	**100 g**
1 cup	**beef stock or consommé**	**250 mL**
1/2 cup	**water if needed**	**125 mL**
	salt and pepper	

Mix all the ingredients together in a soup pot, including the liquid from the beans and the corn. Simmer until the rice and the meat are cooked. Add more water if needed. Season with salt and pepper. This is the sort of soup that can simmer all day in a crock pot if you have one. Just make sure it doesn't go too dry!

Salads,
Dressings
& Dips

Small Bowl Salad for a Potluck

Everywhere we go, we run into places holding potluck suppers! It's a great way to meet new people, taste other people's cooking, and generally have fun. I don't have a bowl in the RV big enough to hold a tossed salad for more than two, so one day I concocted this salad to fit in the bowl I had. It all went at the potluck, and several people came back looking for more. That's the best potluck compliment!

1/2	**onion, minced small**	**1/2**
2	**stalks celery, diced**	**2**
1 can (7 oz)	**corn niblets, drained**	**199 mL**
1 can (7 oz)	**pitted black olives, drained and sliced**	**199 mL**
1/2	**green pepper, diced**	**1/2**
1/4 cup	**olive oil or light vegetable oil**	**50 mL**
2 tbsp	**white wine vinegar**	**25 mL**
1 tsp	**Dijon mustard**	**5 mL**
1/4 tsp	**ground pepper**	**1 mL**
1/4 tsp	**crushed rosemary**	**1 mL**

Prepare the vegetables in a small serving bowl and mix well. Combine the oil, vinegar, mustard, pepper, and rosemary. Mix them well, then pour over the vegetables. You can let this sit with the dressing on for a few hours in the refrigerator if you have the time! Serves six regular servings, or eight to ten at a potluck.

Rally in Peachland, BC

The last weekend in May we spent on the shore of Lake Okanagan, at the rally of SKP chapter 33, the BC Okanagan group. It blew and it rained but we had a good time anyway! I won the first round of the croquet tournament, but lost out on the finals. There was a potluck lunch on Saturday, and a communal BBQ on Sunday. What a great way to eat! This broccoli salad turned up at both those meals. On Saturday Marg Rollins made it with cashews and beautiful big raisins she brought back from California. On Sunday Joyce Roesch made the sunflower seed version. Both times the bowl emptied very quickly!

Broccoli Salad

1/2 cup	mayonnaise	125 mL
3/4 tsp	dry mustard	4 mL
4 tbsp	red wine vinegar	50 mL
2 tbsp	sugar	25 mL
1	bunch broccoli, separated into florets	1
1/2 cup	raisins	125 mL
4 tbsp	chopped red onion	50 mL
3 tbsp	sunflower seeds	45 mL
	OR	
1/2 cup	cashews	125 mL
1/2 lb	bacon fried crisp and crumbled	225 g

Combine the mayonnaise, dry mustard, vinegar, and sugar and mix well. Plump the raisins by soaking them in warm water for 15 minutes or so. Mix together the broccoli, raisins, and onion. For the sunflower seed version, put the seeds in now as well. Pour the dressing over them. Let it stand for several hours, or even overnight. Add the bacon and cashews, if you're using them, at the last minute so they don't get soggy, and mix well.

Cool Salad for Hot Days

To me, citrus fruits and salads are exactly the thing to eat when the weather gets hot. Here's a California salad, to eat south of the walnut groves, where grapefruit and olives grow. I must admit I bought canned olives, and grapefruit and walnuts are available all over the continent, so you could really make this anywhere.

2	**grapefruit, cut into sections**	**2**
1 can (7oz)	**pitted black olives, sliced**	**199 mL**
1/2 cup	**walnut pieces**	**125 mL**
1/4	**head lettuce, torn into bite-sized pieces**	**1/4**
1/4 cup	**olive oil**	**50 mL**
2 tbsp	**white wine vinegar**	**25 mL**
1/2 tsp	**Dijon mustard**	**2 mL**

Put the grapefruit sections, olives, walnuts, and lettuce in a good-sized bowl. Using a fork or whisk, beat the oil, vinegar and mustard in a measuring cup. Pour the dressing over the salad and toss well. Serve as soon as it is dressed. This recipe makes 4 side salads.

April in California

I love mint, as a tea or a sauce for lamb or in a creamy dressing for a salad on a hot day. Southern California in April is hot to me, as hot as June in southern Quebec or Ontario. They say it doesn't feel as hot because of the dryness in the desert areas, but hot is just hot as far as I'm concerned. I made this dressing to go on a carrot and raisin salad with ham kebabs on the barbecue, but it's also good on a leafy green salad or a bowl of cucumbers. Since there's no mayonnaise, it doesn't turn bad in the heat, and there's no fat or salt in it either.

Spicy Mint Dressing

1/2 cup	**nonfat plain yogurt**	**125 mL**
1/2 tsp	**crushed dried mint**	**2 mL**
1/4 tsp	**ground black pepper**	**1 mL**
1/4 tsp	**dried garlic**	**1 mL**

Mix ingredients together in a bowl or measuring cup. Mix well and chill in the refrigerator. If you are using the dressing on a salad without leaves, you may pour it on and chill the salad dressed. For a leafy salad, it's better to add the dressing just before it is served, so that the leaves don't wilt. This makes enough dressing for two servings.

Creamy Raspberry Vinegar Dressing

1/2 cup	**non-fat plain yogurt**	**125 mL**
2 tbsp	**raspberry vinegar**	**25 mL**
1 tbsp	**olive oil**	**15 mL**
	salt, pepper, and sugar to taste	

Combine the ingredients in a bowl or measuring cup, mixing well. This dressing makes a cabbage salad taste quite different and delicious!

Mustard and Tarragon Dip

1/2 cup	**non-fat plain yogurt**	**125 mL**
2 tsp	**Dijon mustard**	**10 mL**
1 tsp	**tarragon**	**5 mL**
2 tsp	**sugar**	**10 mL**
1/4 tsp	**salt**	**1 mL**

Mix all ingredients together well. This is a good dip with fresh veggies such as carrot sticks, celery, green pepper, mushrooms, turnip sticks, broccoli and cauliflower florets. It is a bit thinner than cream cheese dips, but contains a lot less fat! If you like a thicker dip, try mixing yogurt half and half with cream cheese.

Hamburger Relish Dip

This is a surprisingly tasty dip, and extremely simple to make. It comes out thicker than the ones above.

1/2 cup	**hamburger relish**	**125 mL**
1/2 cup	**yogurt**	**125 mL**
1/4 cup	**mayonnaise**	**50 mL**

Mix the ingredients together in a bowl and serve with raw vegetables, chips, or crackers. Since the dip flavor is quite strong, it goes very well with cauliflower or bròccoli. You can substitute your favourite chutney, chili sauce, or even salsa for the hamburger relish.

See the "No Salt, No Fat, No Sugar" section at the end of the book for more salads and dressings.

Meats

By the Cowichan River

Last fall, when we first came to Vancouver Island, the salmon were working their way upstream to spawn. We stopped at the bridge over the Cowichan River to watch the young Indians from the reservation spear fishing. They stood motionless and silent on the supports outside the railings, holding their twelve-foot-long spears, peering down into the water. Dark polarized sunglasses let them see past the sparkling reflections of sunlight where the water shimmered over a gravel bar. A swirl in the shimmer, the arm nearest to me moved, the spear dropped, clanging against the pebbles of the river bottom. The young man hauled it back by the rope attached to his wrist, turned to me, flashed a grin and said, "Too fast." Then he turned back to watch again.

In May we returned to the river and parked on a gravel path just upstream from the bridge. The yellow broom was in flower, and a robin sang nearby. We were tired from a day of errands and driving, so we made a quick simple supper. Later we sat down on the river bank to relax. A pair of trumpeter swans flew by, honking softly to each other, and a swallow swooped low to catch the bugs on the surface of the water. Then I spotted a splash just nearby. Small fish were jumping, completely out of the water! It seemed right that we had beef kebabs for supper, and not salmon that night.

Marinated Beef Kebabs

1/4 lb	**beef stir fry, marinated in teriyaki sauce and cut into 16 equal cubes**	**100 g**
1/2	**green pepper, cut into 8 equal pieces**	**1/2**
1	**medium onion, cut into eighths (see below)**	**1**
4	**mushrooms, cut in halves**	**4**

To cut the onion into eighths that will stay on the skewer, cut it in quarters lengthwise, and then cut each quarter in two the other way. Each piece will have a wide outer layer going down to a wedge in the middle.

Preheat the barbecue. On four skewers, thread a piece of onion, then a piece of meat, then green pepper, then meat, then mushroom, then repeat the pattern starting with another piece of onion. If your meat pieces are large, fold them in half before threading them on the skewer. When the barbecue is hot, turn it down to medium and place the kebabs on the rack. Close the lid, and let them cook for two minutes. Turn them over and cook until the meat is done to your taste. You can turn them several times if need be. Serve with rice or noodles and Yogurt Mustard Sauce (page 71). Serves two.

Hoss Burgers

Donald, one of the co-op members at the Jojoba Hills RV Resort in Aguanga, California, told us about the best burgers he'd ever tasted. They were called Hoss Burgers, from Dolly's Restaurant in Anza, 15 miles away. He said the burgers were huge, and had onions and green peppers mixed in with the meat. So we went to try them out. The burgers were certainly huge, a whole pound of meat, with a correspondingly large bun. Other than that, they were much like the ones I've been making for years. So here's my recipe. I make quarter pounders, since they fit in normal hamburger buns, and serve normal appetites.

Super Burgers, for the Barbecue or Frying Pan

1 lb	**extra lean ground beef**	**450 g**
1	**onion, chopped**	**1**
1/2	**green pepper, chopped**	**1/2**
1	**egg, beaten**	**1**
2 tsp	**Worcestershire sauce**	**10 mL**
1 tsp	**Tabasco sauce**	**5 mL**
1 tsp	**crushed oregano**	**5 mL**
1/4 tsp	**salt**	**1 mL**
1/2 tsp	**ground pepper**	**2 mL**
1 tsp	**sesame or vegetable oil**	**5 mL**
4	**slices cheddar cheese**	**4**
4	**slices Mozzarella cheese**	**4**
1	**tomato**	**1**
	lettuce	
	ketchup, mustard or other sauces	
4	**hamburger buns**	**4**

Preheat the barbecue or frying pan. Put the meat in a bowl. Mix half of the chopped onion, the green pepper, the beaten egg, Worcestershire sauce, Tabasco sauce, oregano, salt and pepper in a separate bowl or measuring cup. Add to the meat. Mix well and form into four patties, pressing them together firmly. The trick to not having burgers fall apart on the barbecue is in shaping the patties so that they aren't too thick in the middle and there's as little air as possible left in. Grease the grill or frying pan with sesame oil or other vegetable oil. Cook the burgers on medium heat, turning only once. If they are thick, remember to let them cook longer than for thin ones. When they are almost done, lay the slices of cheese on top and cover the barbecue or pan to melt the cheese. While the burgers are cooking, slice the tomato and the other half of the onion. Prepare lettuce leaves or chunks. Toast the buns while the cheese is melting. Serve the burgers on the buns, with the tomato, onion, lettuce, and relishes according to each person's taste. This recipe makes four good quarter pounders. How many people that serves is up to your appetites!

Barbecuing near the Grand Canyon

The barbecue is tiny, one of those nice little portable gas jobs, but it's still a trick to find a place to store it. Alex put it all together, and I emptied out the cupboard underneath the refrigerator to make space for it. The plastic bag it came in was big enough to hold the barbecue even with the handles on, so we wrapped it in that to put it away, in case the lava rock crumbles and leaks out the holes. Of course, the bag split eventually. I keep replacing it with a garbage bag, but I think I'll try one of those tough sports bags, if I ever see one at a garage sale. We managed to get a kit from an RV store to connect the barbecue directly to the propane tank on the RV, with a twelve-foot hose so it doesn't have to be right up against the motor home. I'm so glad Alex is good with tools! The little fold-up table that we found abandoned in a campground in New Brunswick is just the right size to hold the barbecue, when we're really boondocking with no picnic tables.

We headed for the Grand Canyon that afternoon, driving for miles up a long straight road through a National Forest. We paid the fee and passed the gate into the Grand Canyon area, then drove some more, wondering when we would see it. I think I expected it to be like approaching mountains, visible for some time before we reached it, but not so. It was more like rushing over a flat plain for hours and hours and coming upon the edge of a hole with no warning Suddenly it was there, right by the side of the road, with just a low stone wall protecting us from flying off into space. We parked and got out, awed by the sheer immensity of it, and by the colours–reds, gold, purple, with dark shadows down the crevices. It is like mountains, only somehow upside down, since ground level is above rather than below. After marvelling at the view and losing track of time completely, we went out of the park and found a great boondocking place in the National Forest just before sunset. Setting up the barbecue only took a minute, and I had the fat hot dogs and buns ready, thinking that, if this didn't work, at least I could cook them up quickly on the stove. It worked out beautifully!

Barbecued Hot Dogs

8	**large hot dogs**	**8**
8	**hot dog buns**	**8**
1/4 lb	**cheddar cheese, sliced thin**	**100 g**
	dill pickles, sliced thin	
	your favourite hot dog garnishes	

Oil the grill and preheat the barbecue. Turn down the heat to low and cook the hot dogs, turning often. Toast the buns two at a time and serve when ready. Tuck slices of cheese around the hotdog and add pickles and relishes. Add a salad, and you've got a satisfying, very simple meal. Serves four.

Lasagna in the Sierra Nevada

After a dusty afternoon driving in a strong wind through the middle of California we turned off and headed up into the hills. Manzanita bushes with smooth dark trunks and grey-green leaves mixed with bush lupins making patches of blue on the hills. We stopped at a place called Coarsegold, and made this complicated (for me!) supper. It was certainly worth the trouble. Note: depending where you are, the sausage may be called kohlbasi, Polish sausage, beef salami, or simply smokies.

4 oz	**lasagna noodles, uncooked**	**100 g**
1/2 lb	**smoked beef sausage, chopped**	**225 g**
1/2	**medium onion, chopped**	**1/2**
1	**clove garlic, minced**	**1**
1 14 oz can	**peeled tomatoes**	**398 mL**
1 5-1/2 oz can	**tomato paste**	**156 mL**
1/2 tsp	**salt**	**2 mL**
1/2 tsp	**oregano**	**2 mL**
1/2 tsp	**crushed chili pepper**	**2 mL**
1/2 tsp	**ground black pepper**	**2 mL**
2 tsp	**sugar**	**10 mL**
1	**egg**	**1**
8 oz	**ricotta cheese**	**225 g**
1/2 tsp	**rosemary**	**2 mL**
1/4 tsp	**salt**	**1 mL**
1 cup	**grated mozzarella cheese**	**250 mL**
1/2 cup	**grated Parmesan cheese**	**125 mL**

Cook lasagna noodles according to package directions. Brown the sausage, onion, and garlic in a large frying pan. Drain off excess fat. Add tomatoes, tomato paste, oregano, salt, pepper, and sugar and simmer for 10 minutes or until well blended. Meanwhile beat the egg in a bowl and add the ricotta cheese, rosemary, and salt. In a square baking pan or a large frying pan with an all-metal handle, layer one-third of the cooked noodles, half of the tomato sauce, half of the ricotta-egg mixture, half of the mozzarella and Parmesan cheeses, then another third of the noodles, the rest of the tomato sauce, the rest of the ricotta-egg mixture, the rest of the noodles and finish with the rest of the grated mozzarella and Parmesan. Bake in the oven at 375° F (190° C) for 30 minutes or until the cheese on the top is melted and browned. This feeds four very nicely.

While you are waiting for the lasagna to bake, start with a salad or crudités with Mustard and Tarragon Dip (see page 49).

Vegetarian Lasagna

In place of the sausage, substitute chopped vegetables, including carrots, zucchini, green peppers, and mushrooms.

Southern California Barbecue

Lamb is one of my favourite meats for barbecuing, particularly the little loin chops. Shoulder chops work well also, and are less expensive. You can marinate the lamb in the minty mixture and also cook it as a sauce if you like, or just make the sauce and barbecue the lamb chops plain. I thought up this recipe while sitting in an RV park in southern California. People around us wanted to know what the great smell was! Barbecuing in a campground or RV park is sometimes a great way to meet new people.

Lamb Chops with Mint Sauce

4	**loin lamb chops**	**4**
	or	
2	**shoulder chops**	**2**
1/4 cup	**sesame oil or other vegetable oil**	**50 mL**
3 tbsp	**red or white wine vinegar**	**45 mL**
1 tsp	**crushed dried mint**	**5 mL**
1/2 tsp	**ground black pepper**	**2 mL**
1	**clove garlic, crushed**	**1**
	or	
1/2 tsp	**dried garlic**	**2 mL**

To marinate the chops: Mix the oil, vinegar and spices together and pour over the chops in a bowl. Cover and chill for at least one hour. Pat the chops dry before barbecuing.

Marinated or not: Preheat the barbecue to heat up the lava rocks. Put the chops on the barbecue and sear on both sides. Then turn the heat down to low and close the lid.

Put the marinade mixture in a small saucepan and bring it to a boil. Allow it to simmer while the chops cook. Taste the sauce and correct the seasonings. You may add a little sugar if it is too tart, and salt and more pepper if you like. Pour the hot sauce over the chops as you serve them. Serves two. Good with potato salad, or with buns and a green salad.

Vancouver Island Beach

Saturday and everyone is on the beach. This beach is on the protected side of Vancouver island, just south of Sidney where the ferries arrive from the mainland. It is littered with logs and twisted pieces of driftwood, but there are few waves, as there's no ocean surf on this side and little wind today. One fellow tries to fly a kite, but it doesn't stay up for long. A family is hosting a birthday party for their daughter, so a crowd of nine and ten-year-old girls play, shrieking in bathing suits on the sand, hair carefully braided down golden tanned backs, while the parents and their friends dispense food and advice. An old mahogany Chris Craft anchors offshore for a while with the awnings down around the back deck and then burbles off quietly to a harbour for the night. At sunset a flock of Canada geese fly by low over the land and sandpipers hunt for food among the bits of seaweed brought in by the tide. Pork chops on the barbecue, with a mixed salad and rolls, make a simple supper for a lazy day.

Barbecued Pork Chops by the Beach

4	**small pork chops**	**4**
1/2 tsp	**steak spice**	**2 mL**
	applesauce	

Preheat the barbecue on high heat. Sprinkle some of the steak spice on the pork chops. Turn the heat down to medium and sear the chops on one side. Turn them over and sprinkle the rest of the steak spice on that side. When both sides are seared turn the heat down to low, and leave the cover on until they are cooked through. You may turn them again if necessary. Serve with applesauce. Ample servings for two.

Out of Gas in the Desert

The other day we ran out of gas in the desert, about five miles east of Desert Center, the nearest gas station. Luckily we'd filled up a gallon container the last time we ran out of gas, in Toronto. You can see that we don't do it often, as that was five thousand miles and seven months ago. Alex poured the gas in and then tried to start the engine. It wouldn't start, so we sat there at the side of the road, as the wind from the passing semi trailers buffeted us. After a few minutes, he tried it again and it went. I figured he'd done something clever to it that I didn't notice, but later he told me he'd just waited. Anyway, it got us to the gas station! Alex loves kebabs! So this recipe is specially for him.

Kebabs with Ham

1/3 lb	**ham steak**	**150 g**
1/4 cup	**teriyaki marinade**	**50 mL**
1/2	**small zucchini, cut into 1 inch chunks**	**1/2**
1/2	**onion, cut into 1 inch chunks**	**1/2**
1/2	**green pepper, cut into 1 inch chunks**	**1/2**
4	**mushrooms, cut into quarters**	**4**

Cut the ham steak into chunks that will fit on the skewer and put the pieces into a bowl. Pour the marinade over them and stir it around so that all the chunks are coated. Cover the bowl and put it in the refrigerator for at least an hour. When you're ready to build the kebabs, cut up the zucchini, onion, and green pepper into chunks that are big enough to stay on. Quarter the mushrooms. Thread the pieces onto four long skewers, alternating the vegetables with the meat pieces. Cook on the barbecue for a total of about six minutes, turning them as needed. Serves two for supper with a salad and corn bread.

Stir Fry with Leftover Pork

Have you ever noticed that pork chops are packaged in threes? I don't know why. This is what I do with that extra one. I cook all three, with rice and a salad, and make sure that I have extra rice left over as well as the extra pork chop. We usually eat all the salad. Then the next day, Alex chops vegetables, and all I have to do is stir fry them with the chopped-up pork chop and rice.

1 tbsp	**butter or margarine**	**15 mL**
1 tbsp	**sesame oil or vegetable oil**	**15 mL**
1/2	**large onion**	**1/2**
1	**clove garlic, minced**	**1**
1	**stalk celery**	**1**
1/2	**green pepper, diced**	**1/2**
1/2 cup	**broccoli florets**	**125 mL**
1	**carrot, sliced**	**1**
4	**mushrooms, sliced**	**4**
1/2	**small zucchini, sliced**	**1/2**
1	**cooked pork chop, cut into small cubes**	**1**
1 cup	**cooked rice**	**250 mL**

Melt the butter or margarine combined with the oil in a frying pan. Add the chopped vegetables and stir fry until they are slightly cooked. Add the pork and the rice and stir fry another five minutes or until the rice is warmed through and the vegetables are soft but not mushy. Makes two hearty servings or three small ones.

Note: You can vary the vegetables used. I like having a carrot or a sweet red pepper in the mixture for colour as well as flavour. This recipe also works with any other kind of leftover meat, poultry, or even fish.

Starting Off to Santa Fe

I made this the first night we spent with Alissa and Mike, in the Evergreen Coho Resort at Chimacum, Washington. They had been living in Vancouver, while we were parked on Vancouver Island. One Sunday they came over to visit us, and moaned about how things weren't turning out as they wanted them to. They really wanted to travel, the way most folks in their early twenties do, but were having trouble getting money together to do it. Alex asked Alissa where she wanted to go and she said Santa Fe, New Mexico. Alex said, "Okay, that sounds good. We'll drive you." Alissa said, "What?" Mike and I both said, "Sure! Why not?" So we did. It was a delightful two weeks that we spent together. They were a great help as recipe testers and dishwashers, and also taught Alex how to play Rummy 500!

Mike and I celebrated our arrival for the very first time in California by insisting on posing for snapshots under the sign on highway number 1. Alissa told us her boss had said that highway was too curvy for motor homes, but we enjoyed the spectacular scenery without a mishap.

Rabbit with Yogurt and Mustard Sauce

1	**rabbit, cut up about 1 3/4 lbs (800 g)**	**1**
1	**clove garlic, minced**	**1**
1/2	**sprig fresh rosemary, minced**	**1/2**
	or	
1/2 tsp	**dried crushed rosemary**	**2 mL**

Heat the oil in a frying pan. Fry the garlic and the rosemary in the oil, then discard carefully, keeping the oil. Brown the rabbit pieces in the flavoured oil. Turn down the heat and cook until tender and juices run clear (about 20 minutes). If you have a cover or second frying pan, cover the pan after the rabbit is browned. Once the rabbit is cooked, remove it to another pan or a plate, and keep it warm in the oven at 200° F (95° C).

Yogurt and Mustard Sauce

1/2	**sprig fresh rosemary, minced**	**1/2**
	or	
1/2 tsp	**dried crushed rosemary**	**2 mL**
2 tsp	**Dijon mustard**	**10 mL**
1/2 cup	**yogurt**	**125 mL**
1 tbsp	**oil**	**15 mL**
1 tbsp	**honey**	**15 mL**

Add the rosemary and the mustard to the pan juices from the rabbit, or whatever other meat you have cooked, and mix in well. Adjust the heat to low and allow the pan to cool down somewhat, stirring to keep the mustard and juices from sticking. Then add the yogurt and stir until smooth. Add the honey and stir some more. Allow to cook until the sauce just starts to bubble. Add salt and pepper to taste. Serve the rabbit pieces (or other meat) with the sauce poured over top.

This makes a festive supper for four with rice and a mixed salad.

Poultry

Spiced-Up Chicken Tenders

In a Phoenix, Arizona supermarket, I bought chicken tenders, which are simply the fillet parts of boneless skinless chicken breast meat. A less expensive alternative uses all the chicken breast meat. Just take chicken breasts and remove the skin. Then carefully cut the meat away from the bone. Trim off any fat and cut the breasts into strips about 1 inch wide. I often use fruit juice instead of wine for sauces, since I rarely have wine on hand. This is the first time I've tried using fresh grapefruit juice, and it really makes this dish taste special! This method also works well with veal, or even pork chops. Sesame oil adds a special flavour too, but you can use vegetable oil instead.

2 tsp	**sesame or vegetable oil**	**10 mL**
1/2 lb	**chicken tenders**	**225 g**
1	**clove garlic, minced**	**1**
1/4	**onion, chopped fine**	**1/4**
	a 1 inch (2.5 cm) piece of fresh ginger, peeled and minced,	
	or	
1 tsp	**powdered ginger**	**5 mL**
1/2 cup	**chopped fresh parsley,**	**125 mL**
	or	
2 tbsp	**crushed dried parsley**	**25 mL**
	juice of half a pink grapefruit	
	or	
1/4 cup	**white wine**	**50 mL**

Heat the oil in a stir fry pan and add the chicken pieces. Sear them on both sides, turning until all the outsides looked partly cooked. Then add the garlic, onion, ginger, and parsley and turn the heat down. Stir and cook for about 10 minutes, until the chicken is cooked through and the flavours have melded. Remove the chicken pieces with whatever bits of vegetables stick to them. Add the grapefruit juice or wine to what's left in the pan and turn the heat to high. Scrape the goodies off the bottom of the pan and allow the sauce to bubble until reduced about half. Put the chicken pieces back in the pan and turn them to cover with the sauce. When you serve them, pour the remains of the sauce over the chicken. Serves two for supper with rice and a salad.

Santa Fe Rest Stop Supper

We made this dish at a rest stop just outside of Santa Fe in New Mexico when travelling with Mike and Alissa. New Mexico has the nicest rest stops I've seen yet for boondockers. The one outside Santa Fe on Highway I25 has spaces for RVs behind the building so we were a little way from the traffic noise, with picnic tables in shelters, a dumping station, and a clean water tap. There's a big sign that says if you park for more than twenty-four hours, you may be liable to a fine of up to a hundred dollars. So we stayed overnight and went in to Santa Fe in the morning. The funny thing was that when we woke up at six a.m., all the other RVers had already hit the road! We lounged around and had poached eggs for breakfast, emptied the holding tanks, filled the water tank, and got the local paper from the box beside the rest rooms before pulling out at twenty after eight.

Barbecued Chicken Breasts for Four

4	**boneless skinless chicken breasts**	4
1/2 cup	**teriyaki marinade**	125 mL
1	**tomato, sliced**	1
	lettuce	
	creamy raspberry vinegar dressing	
4	**large sesame seed hamburger buns**	4
	mustard	

In the morning, put the chicken breasts in a bowl or plastic container and cover with the marinade. Leave in the refrigerator all day.

When you're ready to start cooking, preheat the barbecue so that the lava rocks are hot. Oil the rack with a small amount of sesame or other oil. Sear the chicken breasts on both sides and then turn the gas down to its lowest setting and close the lid. The chicken will take about 10 minutes to cook and may be turned over halfway through. Slice the tomato, prepare lettuce and the dressing. Remove the chicken from the barbecue when cooked and toast the buns. Slice the chicken breasts. Each person builds his or her own bunwich of chicken, tomato, lettuce, mustard, and dressing. Serves four.

The variations on this recipe are limited only by your taste and imagination! Slices of onion, mushrooms, green or red pepper rings, salsa, guacamole, and any other garnishes you prefer can be used.

Pelicans and Dolphins

I'd never seen pelicans or dolphins before, only pictures of them. Last night we stopped at the Rincon Parkway off Highway 101 near Ventura California, and saw both. The parkway is built alongside the old highway, right above the beach on the Pacific Ocean. It's boondocking, and costs eleven dollars a night, which seemed a bit pricey at first. We realized that our choice was to stay there, or go and sit in some garage parking lot, as we'd broken the main leaf on one of the springs at the back of the motor home. We were ready for a night at the beach after three weeks in the desert or near desert, so we decided to stay and look for a garage in the morning. We levelled up the motor home as best we could, and put out the awning and the chairs.

Then I noticed the pelicans. They are huge ungainly looking birds, until they fly. Then they are beautiful to watch! They sail on the air, then suddenly turn and tuck in their wings. They shoot down into the ocean, causing a spume of spray to rise, then sit back up on the top of the next wave, with lunch in their beaks. They ride there to chew, then stretch their neck out full length for the swallow and are up on wings again. I watched one flying low to the water along the troughs of the waves just before they broke. It seemed his wing tips must touch the wave and send him off balance, but he lifted just in time and slid over into the next trough. Later we saw three of them playing follow the leader just before the sun set, dipping and circling, and coasting along the troughs. They were so graceful against the orange of the sky!

The dolphins? They arrived about half an hour after we did, swimming parallel to the coast and just beyond the first breaking wave. They rose and showed their fins, then plunged back down below the surface, not going terribly fast, and swimming quite close to each other in twos or threes. This morning they came back and showed us how they surf, playing in the waves, riding the crests or diving through them. It felt so joyful, watching them!

Alex and I played in the surf too, laughing as the waves surged in around our ankles, then threatened to overbalance us as the water flowed back out. Afterwards we climbed up the rocks to our parking spot and lit the barbecue for supper. I hadn't planned anything particular, so I pulled four little tortillas out of the freezer and checked my vegetable drawer. Here's what I came up with, which Alex pronounced very good .

California Kebabs for the Beach

1	**onion, cut in twelve chunks**	**1**
1/2	**green pepper, cut in twelve chunks**	**1/2**
6	**mushrooms, cut in half**	**6**
4	**slices smoked turkey**	**4**
4	**corn tortillas**	**4**
1/2 cup	**grated mozzarella cheese**	**125 mL**

Light the barbecue and let it preheat while you prepare the kebabs. Prepare the vegetables. Cut the turkey slices in thirds lengthwise and roll up the pieces. Take four skewers and thread the onion, mushroom, green pepper, and turkey. Turn the barbecue down to medium and put the kebabs on, cooking them with the lid almost closed and turning them frequently. When they are almost done, push them together to make room for the tortillas. Lay the tortillas on the grill and toast one side. Then turn them over and sprinkle grated mozzarella on each one. Cook until the cheese is melted. Put two tortillas on each plate and strip the kebabs onto them. Garnish with salsa, sour cream or anything else you want to add. Wrap the tortilla around the kebab food and eat with your fingers. A delicious light supper for two!

Turkey Breast in Soy Marinade

1	**turkey breast**	**1**
1/2 cup	**soy sauce**	**125 mL**
1/2 cup	**water**	**125 mL**
1 tsp	**garlic powder**	**5 mL**
1 tsp	**ground ginger**	**5 mL**
1 tbsp	**oil**	**15 mL**

Slice the turkey breast into thick strips. Combine the soy sauce, water, garlic powder, and ginger in a bowl. Marinate the turkey in it for an hour or longer. Heat the oil in the frying pan. Cook the turkey strips, turning them to brown all sides. It will only take a few minutes to cook them. If you leave them too long, they'll get tough! Serves two.

A Happy Ending to the Spring Problem

The broken spring? Well, Alex jacked up the back and put a piece of wood in to keep the frame up off the axle, and we drove in to Santa Barbara. Of course there was no one there who did springs, but a few phone calls to truck repair places listed in the Yellow Pages got us a referral to a spring specialist up in Orcutt, about seventy miles north. We called and they assured us they could fix it, so we set off up the 101 through beautiful rolling farm country. No loud bangs along the way, and now we're sitting in this little town, while they repair the spring. I thought I might have to walk back a couple of miles to the bank machine to get cash to pay, but they take credit cards, so I relax and write this instead.

Fish &
Seafood

Engine Troubles Revisited

Did you ever have the experience of thinking things were just going too smoothly for reality and then hit a patch where everything seemed to go wrong? Well, that's what happened to us, around the weekend we spent on Vancouver Island with our friend Bonnie. She's the one who likes those crazy peanut butter sandwiches.

A few days after we left her at the ferry, the engine problem wasn't really gone, even though the terrible noise stopped. Less and less power going up hills, and then the noise came back. Something had to be done! Luckily we weren't in a hurry to get anywhere, so we just stopped and wondered what to do. The answer showed up, as answers sometimes do. Alex explained the problem to a man we met, and he told us to call someone he knew who had a small mechanic's shop behind his house. We ended up limping down Cedar Road. outside of Nanaimo, not quite sure of directions. When we phoned, Len told us we were just around the corner from his place, and to come right over. He and his wife had just come back from crabbing over at Port Renfrew on the west coast of the island. The welcome we received was wonderful–fresh cooked crab and friendship on the back porch. We stayed in their backyard for two days while Len and Alex took the engine apart and put it back together. Marg taught me the secret of cooking fresh crab. It really does taste a lot better than the canned variety!

Boiled Fresh Crab

fresh caught crabs
sea water sufficient to cover the crabs you have

Split the crab open and remove the innards before you cook them. That's the first trick. The second part is to use sea water to cook them. Bring the sea water to a boil, put the crabs in, and cover. Cook until the meat comes loose from the shell, which takes just a few minutes. Serve as is, or with melted butter or margarine and lemon juice. If you're not by the ocean, you'll have to steam them instead. Even if the crab gets flown fresh to wherever you are, I doubt that anyone flies in the sea water for cooking them!

Ocean to Ocean

We really did go from the Atlantic to the Pacific on our travels, so Maine came long before Vancouver Island, but crab comes before lobster if we're doing things alphabetically! In Biddeford, Maine, I wanted lobster, but I didn't know how I would cook it. The pot I have might hold a crab cut in half, but it certainly wouldn't do for a lobster! There was a little shack with a big fresh seafood sign covering the side wall, so I went to investigate. The fish seller had the answer. He sold me four precooked lobster tails, and told me how to heat them. Of course, I could have made a salad of them, but I wanted them hot, with garlic toast, melted butter, and a green side salad. This makes for a high fat combination, but I only indulge this way once or twice a year.

Maine Lobster Tails

4	**lobster tails, precooked**	**4**
1/4 cup	**melted butter**	**50 mL**

Boil a small amount of water in the bottom of a steamer. When the water is boiling hard, put the lobster tails in to steam, two at a time. Don't leave them in too long, as they'll get tough. Serve with the melted butter or margarine for dipping, and garlic toast (see the Snacks section).

NOTE: You could probably reheat them in the microwave as well, but I haven't tried it, so I can't say if they'd toughen up that way or not.

Seasoned Crumb Coated Fish Fillets

This is a mixture that my mother would love. She always liked to use crackers for coating fish fillets. I do this with any white fish fillets I can get, bass, pickerel or pike from fresh water lakes, red snapper, halibut or even sole from the sea. The main thing about fish is the fresher the better!

10	**crackers**	**10**
1/2 tsp	**dried parsley flakes**	**2 mL**
1/2 tsp	**dried tarragon**	**2 mL**
1/2 tsp	**ground black pepper**	**2 mL**
1/4 tsp	**dried garlic**	**1 mL**
1	**egg, beaten**	**1**
1 tbsp	**milk or water**	**15 mL**
1 tbsp	**safflower or vegetable oil**	**15 mL**
1/2 lb	**white fish fillets**	**225 g**

Take a clean plastic bag big enough to hold a fillet of fish with space left over. Put the crackers in the bag and crush them with a rolling pin, an empty bottle, or the heel of your hand until they resemble coarse bread crumbs. Add the parsley, tarragon, pepper, and garlic and shake the bag to mix them with the cracker crumbs. Beat the egg and milk in a bowl. Heat the oil in a frying pan. When the oil is hot, take each fillet in turn, dip it in the egg and then toss it in the crumb mixture. Fry on both sides, but not too long. Serves two nicely.

California Coast Revisited

We left Chico and headed for the coast of northern California. Highway 299 winds through spectacular mountains with long hills and breathtaking views of the Trinity River and various creeks. When we got down to McKinleyville, I stopped to replenish our larder. There were lovely plump scallops in the supermarket display. The fellow behind the counter said, yes, they had been frozen, so I bought some.

Usually I prefer to buy fresh, but I know now that the frozen ones are processed as soon as possible after they come out of the sea, so they're often fresher than the fresh ones, particularly in a supermarket. I just wanted seafood right away, to celebrate reaching the sea again.

We drove up the coast a little way out of town, and found a spot to park, a dune away from the beach. We both napped for an hour and then cooked supper together. Alex put the water on for the rice, and chopped the vegetables. He still doesn't realize that that's three-quarters of the work of making a stir fry supper! I like to use a combination of butter and safflower or other vegetable oil for dishes with seafood, as it doesn't taste as strong as the sesame oil that I usually use for cooking meat or chicken.

Scallop Stir Fry

1 tbsp	**butter or margarine**	**15 mL**
1 tbsp	**safflower or vegetable oil**	**15 mL**
1	**onion, chopped**	**1**
1/2	**green pepper, diced**	**1/2**
1	**stick celery, chopped**	**1**
1	**broccoli, separated into florets**	**1**
8	**mushrooms, sliced**	**8**
1/4 lb	**scallops, thawed if previously frozen**	**100 g**

Melt the butter or margarine and heat the oil in the pan. Add the vegetables and stir fry until practically cooked. Remove them to a bowl, and sauté the scallops in the pan. You may serve them separately, or put the vegetables back in the pan and mix them with the scallops. Serve with rice. Serves two generously.

Vegetarian
Dishes

A Question of Weight

I realized that all the cans I had in the cupboard were adding a bit to the weight of our rig. At the Escapade seminars we had learned that fifty-eight percent of RVs are overweight, which is hard on the suspension system, and on the tires. So I decided to use up some of the cans. This recipe turned out to be enough for two suppers for the two of us, and reduced my cupboard contents by four cans! Of course, that didn't make a big difference for the suspension, but it made me feel better, anyway. The sauce turned out to be quite delicious, and has the advantage of containing no added fat.

No-Fat Pasta Sauce

1 can (14 oz)	**whole peeled tomatoes, broken up**	**398 mL**
1 can (14 oz)	**lima beans, drained**	**398 mL**
1 can (12 oz)	**kernel corn, drained**	**341 mL**
1 can (7 oz)	**pitted black olives, drained and sliced**	**199 mL**
2 tsp	**Worcestershire sauce**	**10 mL**
1/2 tsp	**Tabasco sauce**	**2 mL**
1	**onion, chopped**	**1**
1/2 tsp	**dried crushed oregano**	**2 mL**
1/4 tsp	**pepper**	**1 mL**

Put all ingredients together in a saucepan. Bring the mixture to the boil and then turn it down to simmer. Simmer for at least half an hour, with the lid off. If you want to make it thicker, use 1 tbsp (15 mL) cornstarch mixed with a little cold water to thicken it. Continue boiling the sauce after adding the cornstarch for 2 or 3 minutes, until the sauce thickens and the cornstarch is incorporated. Meanwhile cook the noodles, or other pasta. This makes enough for four people for one meal, or two people twice.

Ferry Ride to Vancouver Island

We came across to Vancouver Island on the brand new ferry called the *Spirit of Vancouver Island*. I went out on the front of the upper deck, just under the bridge, and found a protected spot partly out of the wind. The air was crystal clear, the sort of day that makes the trees on the Gulf Islands seem touchable. A fin rose from the water, just off the bow, and then another and another. It was a pod of young killer whales, who surfaced and then surged out of the water as we glided past. I fell in love with the islands all over again.

Later we called my niece Patti in Victoria, who was expecting a baby any day, and offered to bring dinner. She was delighted, so we bought some vegetables and noodles and made pasta and a colourful vegetable sauce with fresh fennel from her garden. You can certainly use dried fennel instead.

Pasta Sauce for Patti

2 tsp	**olive oil**	**10 mL**
1	**onion, chopped**	**1**
1	**sweet red pepper, chopped**	**1**
1/2	**green pepper, chopped**	**1/2**
1/2 lb	**mushrooms, sliced**	**225 g**
2	**stalks celery, chopped**	**2**
3 tbsp	**fresh fennel, minced**	**45 mL**
	or	
1 tbsp	**dried fennel**	**15 mL**
2 tsp	**butter or margarine**	**10 mL**
2 tbsp	**flour**	**25 mL**
1 cup	**milk**	**250 mL**
1 cup	**grated mozzarella cheese**	**250 mL**

Heat the oil in a large frying pan and sauté the vegetables, stirring with a wooden spoon. Add the fennel and stir. Remove the vegetables to a bowl. Turn down the heat under the frying pan to low. Melt the butter or margarine in the pan, and sprinkle the flour on it. Stir well. Add the milk gradually, stirring it in with the butter-flour mixture. Smooth out any lumps with the wooden spoon. Cook until the milk just starts to bubble and the sauce begins to thicken. Add the cheese and keep stirring until the cheese is blended in. Now put the vegetables back in the pan and stir to coat them with the sauce. Serve on noodles or fusilli. Serves four.

Pepper Trees

The trees around the old house at Jojoba Hills are tall with feathery leaves and clusters of bright pink berries. I thought at first those were the flowers, but realized that the flowers are white, and the pink clusters are tiny berry pods. It took a week before I made the connection with remarks about how easy it is to care for pepper trees. Those bright pink berries are pepper berries, just like the ones in the pepper mills at fancy restaurants in Toronto. Pink and green pepper berries are softer than the black or white ones, and a bit less fiery, but they still pack a punch, particularly when they're fresh. Here's a pasta sauce that I made while watching the quails strut beneath the pepper trees, pecking at the ground. I don't know if they were eating pepper berries or not! In any case, with whatever colour of pepper you have on hand, this makes a delicious simple supper for two.

Vegetable and Mozzarella Pasta Sauce

1 tbsp	**olive oil**	**15 mL**
1	**onion, chopped**	**1**
6	**large mushrooms, chopped**	**6**
1/2	**green pepper, chopped**	**1/2**
1/2	**sweet red pepper, chopped**	**1/2**
2 tbsp	**flour**	**25 mL**
1/2 cup	**milk**	**125 mL**
1 cup (or more)	**grated mozzarella cheese**	**250 mL**
1/4 tsp	**ground pepper, red, green, white, or black**	**1 mL**
1 tsp	**dried crushed tarragon**	**5 mL**

Heat the olive oil in a frying pan and sauté the vegetables in it. When they are partially cooked, sprinkle them with the flour and stir until the flour disappears. Turn the heat down to low and add the milk. Stir and let it cook until the mixture bubbles a bit around the edges. Stir in the cheese until it melts and gets blended in. Add the pepper and tarragon and stir again. Allow the sauce to simmer until you are ready to serve it over cooked pasta. This serves two.

Birds, Known and Unknown

I sat outside the motor home at Jojoba Hills in the shade and watched birds yesterday. They made the most glorious sounds and I knew I was in a foreign place. I counted ten different species that flew past, or walked between the bushes down below my hilltop vantage point, and I knew a name for only one of them. That one was a hummingbird, but even he was coloured differently from the ruby-throated ones I know from eastern Canada. This one had a totally iridescent red head. When he turned and his feathers caught the sun, his whole head glowed. The folks next door to us had a feeder for them, and six of them came at one time to sip the sugar water. I tried taking photographs of them, but it was hard to catch them at the right moment to see the colours!

There was another bird, about the size of a robin but with a much longer tail, that had three different shades of blue, as well as some black and white, on his head, wings, and tail. I realized that not knowing their names actually made me observe them more closely, and enjoy them more than I did the birds back home.

Similarly, I've got interested in Mexican-type cooking. There are in the supermarkets here all sorts of beans and tortillas and sauces , which I don't really know what to do with, but I bought some anyway and started experimenting. This is one of the successful outcomes!

Tortillas with Beans

1 can (14 oz)	**beans with jalapeno peppers**	**398 mL**
1 cup	**grated cheddar cheese**	**250 mL**
1	**tomato**	**1**
6	**lettuce leaves**	**6**
6	**small corn tortillas**	**6**
1/2 cup	**nonfat yogurt (or sour cream)**	**125 mL**
12	**pitted sliced black olives (optional)**	**12**
1/4	**onion, chopped (optional)**	**1/4**

Heat the beans in a pot on the stove. Lay the tortillas on a cookie sheet and heat them under the broiler. Turn them over when the top side is hot and crisp but not too brown. Chop the tomato. Tear the lettuce into bite-sized pieces. Put the tortillas on two plates, spoon the beans over them, cover with grated cheese, tomato, and lettuce. Garnish with a dollop of yogurt or sour cream. You can also add sliced black olives and chopped onion if you wish. Ample servings for two.

Desserts

Mountain Road

Maps are very deceiving! After we left Santa Fe, we went south and then turned west near Truth or Consequences. What a surprise when the desert turned into mountains in the Gila National Forest. The road wound around and around and up and up. We rumbled over a cattle guard past a sign saying Livestock on Road and continued climbing. It was great to see trees again and, yes, we did find some livestock! The cows eyed us and walked on. Then we coasted down into Arizona, where the land flattened out again.

On Easter Sunday we arrived at the SKP resort in Benson, Arizona where they were having a potluck Easter Sunday dinner. It took me half the day to find the person in charge, who asked me to bring a dessert. I had an hour to make it! So I put together a yogurt strawberry fool, which didn't set. It tasted great though, so that was okay, and it paid our way in to a sumptuous dinner. Next time, I'll use whipped cream and make a proper fool of myself, and keep this recipe for serving over cake.

Sloppy Strawberry Fool

2 cups	**fresh strawberries**	**500 mL**
1 cup	**plain yogurt**	**250 mL**
2 tbsp	**sugar**	**25 mL**

Wash, hull, and chop the strawberries. Mash them with a masher if you have one, or a fork if you don't. They'll probably still be a bit lumpy. Add the yogurt and the sugar and mix well. Chill for at least an hour.

Proper Strawberry Fool

2 cups	**fresh strawberries**	**500 mL**
1/2 cup	**whipping cream**	**125 mL**
1 tbsp	**sugar, or to taste**	**15 mL**

Wash and hull the strawberries. Keep out four particularly nice ones for garnish. Purée the rest of the berries in a blender if you have one, or mash them through a sieve. Whip the cream and add the sugar. Fold the berry purée into the sweetened whipped cream. Spoon into individual serving dishes or a pretty serving bowl. Chill for an hour or more. Just before you serve it, garnish with the reserved berries. Serves four.

Mango and Citrus Fruit Salad

Fruit salad is wonderful on a hot day, either for breakfast in place of orange juice, for lunch with cottage cheese, or as a supper dessert with yogurt or ice cream. In my opinion, every fruit salad should start with citrus fruits partly because the citric acid will keep all the other additions (in this case the mango) from going brown. I made this on an April Saturday morning in California, when the temperature was predicted to go over 90° F. That way I didn't have to produce anything special later in the day!

4	**small oranges**	**4**
2	**grapefruit**	**2**
1	**mango**	**1**
1/4 cup	**raisins**	**50 mL**
1/4 cup	**chopped walnuts**	**50 mL**

Peel and slice the oranges, cutting the slices in half and removing all the seeds. Be sure to remove the white part of the skin, as it is bitter. Put the orange slices in a bowl. Section the grapefruit, remove the seeds, and add the sections and the grapefruit juice to the oranges. Peel a ripe mango and cut the flesh off the stone. Chop into bite-sized pieces. Mix it in with the citrus fruit. Add raisins and walnuts and chill until ready to serve.

Citrus Section Salad

We drove through Quartzsite, Arizona in early April, but the season was already over. There were a few trailers and motor homes dotting the landscape, but most of the areas were just empty lots with blowing dust. On the side of the road, two men were selling grapefruit and oranges from their pickup truck. I bought eight grapefruit and a dozen oranges for two dollars. Then I wondered what to do with them!

1	**grapefruit**	**1**
2	**oranges**	**2**
1/4 cup	**raisins and walnut pieces**	**50 mL**

Section the grapefruit and the oranges. Put the sections in a bowl with the raisins and nuts. Squeeze the remaining juice out of the grapefruit and orange halves into the bowl. Add the raisins and nuts and mix well. You may eat this right away, or chill it in the refrigerator for later. Serves two.

Pineapple Cream Pie

This recipe came from one of Alex's sisters-in-law. While we were visiting his family in Calgary, four of his brothers got Alex involved building a new fence for their mother's yard. After lunch, while they all went back to their hammers and levels, Mary gave me this recipe to add to the book. Even though she's not an RVer, her recipe suits my little kitchen on wheels very well. It's simple, delicious, and good looking too! Who knows; maybe Mary and Clarence will try the RV life too.

1	**graham cracker pie crust**	**1**
8 oz	**cream cheese**	**225 g**
1/4 cup	**sugar**	**50 mL**
8 oz	**Cool Whip**	**225 g**
	or	
1/4 cup	**whipping cream, whipped**	**50 mL**
1 can (14 oz)	**crushed pineapple**	**398 mL**
	nuts and/or maraschino cherries to garnish (optional)	

Beat the sugar into the cream cheese, then fold in the whipped cream or Cool Whip. Drain the crushed pineapple and mix it in. Spoon into the pie crust and chill for at least half an hour. You may garnish this with nuts and/or maraschino cherries to make it look really festive.

Baking

Las Vegas Stop

On our trip to Santa Fe, we stopped at Las Vegas, partly because neither Mike nor I had ever been there, and partly because Alissa's aunt and uncle had invited us to their house to stay. Mike and Alissa took full advantage of the invitaion, and slept in the house. Alex and I stayed in the motor home parked outside, and came in for meals, baths, and sociability. Aunt Marlene and Uncle Steve were tremendously hospitable, giving us good advice as to what to see, insights into the backstage part of the Strip, and these muffins for breakfast. It was a great weekend, even though I didn't win any money.

Las Vegas Apple Oat Bran Muffins

2 cups	**oat bran**	**500 mL**
1/2 cup	**sugar**	**125 mL**
2 tsp	**baking powder**	**10 mL**
1 tsp	**cinnamon**	**5 mL**
1/2 tsp	**salt**	**2 mL**
1 cup	**low-fat milk**	**250 mL**
2	**egg whites**	**2**
2 tbsp	**Canola oil or vegetable oil**	**25 mL**
2 tbsp	**molasses**	**25 mL**
3/4 cup	**applesauce (unsweetened)**	**175 mL**
1/2 cup	**raisins**	**125 mL**
1/2 cup	**walnuts**	**125 mL**

Put all ingredients in a large bowl. Mix by hand just until combined. Spoon into papered muffin pan, filling each full, using all the batter. Bake 16 minutes at 425° F (220° C). Makes 12 muffins.

Note: The applesauce in the muffins adds moistness and reduces the amount of fat (oil and egg yolks) required.

Pumpkin Muffins

Here's another recipe from the SKPs of the Okanagan in British Columbia. As part of their rally, they had a recipe swap, so I picked up several good ideas. The broccoli salad in the salad section is one, and here's another. If you have a source of fresh pumpkin, boil it and mash it and use it instead of the canned kind. Of course, that's only possible in October in Canada, so for the rest of the year, use canned!

4	**eggs**	**4**
2 cups	**sugar**	**500 mL**
1 1/2 cups	**oil**	**375 mL**
1 can (14 oz)	**pumpkin**	**398 mL**
3 cups	**flour**	**750 mL**
1 tbsp	**cinnamon**	**15 mL**
2 tsp	**baking soda**	**10 mL**
2 tsp	**baking powder**	**10 mL**
1 tsp	**salt**	**5 mL**
2 cups	**raisins**	**500 mL**

Beat the eggs, and beat in the sugar, oil, and pumpkin. In a separate bowl, stir together the flour, cinnamon, baking soda, and baking powder. Add to the liquid ingredients and blend until smooth. Stir in the raisins. Fill greased or lined muffin tins 2/3 full. Bake 15 minutes at 400° F (205° C). Makes 24.

Journey Cake near the Mexican Border

Traveling through New Mexico, Arizona, and southern California, I am amazed at the changes in landscape, from mountains covered with huge Sequoia pines to dusty hot desert floors where only huge cacti and Desert Candles flourish. Each area has its birds and animals. Roadrunners speed along the top of the wall behind our motor home near Casa Grande, Arizona. They are so much bigger than I expected! The food stores have whole aisles devoted to Mexican food, refried beans, chili con carne, varieties of peppers fresh, dried and canned, about which I know nothing. I buy a box of cornmeal, and vow to eat someone else's bean and pepper concoctions before trying to make my own. All I can do is make corn bread, for now. Later I find out that another name for cornmeal bread is Johnnycake, which is a corruption of Journey Cake. No wonder I like it so much!

Corn Bread (also called Johnnycake or Journey Cake)

1 cup	**yellow cornmeal**	**250 mL**
1 cup	**flour**	**250 mL**
1/4 cup	**sugar**	**50 mL**
1 tbsp	**baking powder**	**15 mL**
1 tsp	**salt**	**5 mL**
1/2 cup	**oil**	**125 mL**
1	**egg**	**1**
1 cup	**milk**	**250 mL**

Preheat the oven to 400° F (205° C). Combine dry ingredients in a bowl and mix well. Combine liquid ingredients in another bowl or measuring cup and mix well. Stir the wet into the dry until just blended. Pour into a well-greased 8 inch square (20 cm by 20 cm) baking pan or frying pan with an ovenproof handle. Bake for 25 minutes or until the top springs back when you press it lightly. Serve warm with butter or margarine or with a creamed main dish such as chicken or fish.

Posh in Chemainus

The folks who introduced us to the Escapees club are now settled on Vancouver Island, having opened a little cafe in Chemainus, called the Posh Deli and Catering Company. One of Sharon's specialties is cheese scones. She gave me the recipe and I discovered that it's quite possible to make them in the RV oven. One trick that I found useful: if your oven tends to burn the bottom of things, wrap a piece of aluminum foil around the shelf underneath the baking pan. That way your scones can get nicely brown on top without getting black on the bottom. Sharon and Bill are hoping to get back on the road in a couple of years but, in the meantime, if you're in Chemainus, drop in to Posh for lunch!

Grandma Sharon's Scones

2 cups	**all-purpose flour**	**500 mL**
1/2 cup	**sugar**	**125 mL**
1 tsp	**salt**	**5 mL**
4 tsp	**baking powder**	**20 mL**
1/4 cup	**shortening**	**50 mL**
1/2 cup	**grated orange cheddar cheese**	**125 mL**
2/3 cup	**milk**	**150 mL**

Sift the dry ingredients together (or mix them together with a fork if you don't have a sifter). Cut in the shortening as if you were making pastry. Add the cheese and stir in the milk. Turn out onto a floured board and knead the dough. Pat it down to about 1/4 inch (1/2 cm) thick. Cut into eight equal pieces and form each piece into a round. Place them on a greased baking sheet and bake until nicely browned (about 15 minutes) at 450° F (230° C). These are great hot for breakfast or with soup for lunch, or even for tea!

Variation: For raisin scones, use 1/2 cup (125 mL) raisins and no cheese.

Herbed Baking Powder Biscuits (sugar-free)

2 cups	**flour**	**500 mL**
1/2 tsp	**salt**	**2 mL**
4 tsp	**baking powder**	**20 mL**
1 tsp	**dried parsley flakes**	**5 mL**
1 tsp	**dried crushed savoury**	**5 mL**
1 tsp	**dried whole thyme**	**5 mL**
1/2 cup	**shortening or lard**	**125 mL**
2/3 cup	**milk**	**150 mL**

Preheat the oven to 425° F (220° C). Grease a cookie sheet. Mix the dry ingredients in a bowl. Cut in the shortening until the mixture resembles coarse breadcrumbs. Add the milk all at once, and mix just until it sticks together. Turn out on a floured board and knead lightly. Pat it down to 1/2 inch (1 cm) thick. Cut into rounds. I use the ring from a mason jar for a cutter, but a juice glass works as well. Place the rounds on the cookie sheet. Bake 12 to 15 minutes, until golden brown. Serve immediately! This makes 12 biscuits.

Cookies for Small Kids and Big Ones Too

Grandmothers always make cookies, don't they? Two ladies at Jojoba Hills make them every morning and take them up the hill to where the other folks are working, along with a canteen of fresh coffee strapped to the back of the golf cart. Several of these recipes are from their recipe box. When it came time to test them, I was in Calgary visiting Alex's grandchildren, Ashley and Sean. So I enlisted their help in both making and eating the cookies. They couldn't decide which ones they liked best, but they both loved cleaning the batter out of the bowls!

Old-Fashioned Peanut Butter Cookies

Ashley and Sean love these ones, and they're easy to make. Make sure you leave plenty of space on the cookie sheet for them to spread, because they will!

1/2 cup	**butter or margarine**	**125 mL**
1/2 cup	**peanut butter (smooth or crunchy)**	**125 mL**
1/2 cup	**white sugar**	**125 mL**
1/2 cup	**brown sugar**	**125 mL**
1	**egg, beaten**	**1**
1/2 tsp	**vanilla**	**2 mL**
1 cup	**flour**	**250 mL**
1/2 tsp	**salt**	**2 mL**
1/2 tsp	**baking soda**	**2 mL**

Preheat the oven to 350° F (180° C). and grease your cookie sheet(s). Cream the butter or margarine and peanut butter together. Beat in the sugar. Add the egg and vanilla and mix well. Combine the flour, salt, and baking soda. Add the dry ingredients to the peanut butter mixture and mix until it's smooth. Form into 1 inch (2.5 cm) balls and place at least 1 inch (2.5 cm) apart on the cookie sheets. Press down with the tines of a wet fork. Bake for about 7 minutes. Makes about 48 cookies.

Orange-Oatmeal-Coconut Cookies

2 cups	**flour**	**500 mL**
2 cups	**sugar**	**500 mL**
4 tsp	**baking powder**	**20 mL**
1 tsp	**salt**	**5 mL**
1 tsp	**nutmeg**	**5 mL**
1 cup	**margarine or oil**	**250 mL**
2	**eggs**	**2**
4 tbsp	**grated orange rind**	**50 mL**
2 tbsp	**orange juice**	**25 mL**
2 cups	**quick cooking oats**	**500 mL**
2 cups	**coconut**	**500 mL**

Sift flour, sugar, baking powder, salt, and nutmeg in a large mixing bowl. Add margarine, eggs, orange rind, orange juice, oats, and coconut, mixing well after each ingredient is added. Drop onto greased cookie sheet. Bake at 350° F (180° C) until lightly brown. Makes 48 to 60 dozen.

Fudgy Brownies

Alex's daughter, Chantal, liked these the best of all. So I gave her a bag of the mix, along with the recipe.

Make-Ahead Brownie Mix

8 cups	**sugar**	**2 l**
5 1/2 cups	**flour**	**1350 mL**
3 cups	**cocoa**	**750 mL**
4 tsp	**baking powder**	**20 mL**
2 tsp	**salt**	**10 mL**

Stir until well mixed. Store in tight container. Enough for several batches of brownies.

Brownies

2 cups	**mix**	**500 mL**
1/2 cup	**margarine, melted**	**125 mL**
2	**eggs**	**2**
1/2 cup	**nuts, chopped**	**125 mL**
1 tsp	**vanilla**	**5 mL**

Blend ingredients and mix 2 minutes. Bake in 8 inch square pan at 350° F (180° C) for 25 minutes.

Banana Nut Bars

These are Alex's favourites. They are quite sweet.

1/2 cup	**shortening**	**125 mL**
2	**eggs**	**2**
1 cup	**sugar**	**250 mL**
1 1/2 cups	**flour**	**375 mL**
1/2 tsp	**baking soda**	**2 mL**
1/2 tsp	**salt**	**2 mL**
1/3 cup	**milk**	**75 mL**
1 tsp	**lemon juice**	**5 mL**
1	**very ripe banana, mashed**	**1**
1/2 cup	**chopped nuts.**	**125 mL**

Beat the shortening, eggs, and sugar well. Add the flour, baking soda, salt, milk, lemon juice, banana, and nuts, mixing well after each addition. Bake in a greased 9 x 13 inch (23 x 33 cm) pan at 350° F (180° C) for 25 to 30 minutes. Cool in the pan.

No-Salt, No-Fat,
No-Sugar Recipes

Many of the folks I met on the road were following special diets to help stave off various medical problems. So I have developed some recipes with them in mind. Their courage and enthusiasm for life is contagious! Of course, this doesn't mean that you can't enjoy these recipes if you're not on a special diet. Some things are good for all of us. Certain ideas I've used here can also be adapted to other recipes. I look on cooking with special restrictions as a challenge, and allow myself to experiment. It doesn't always turn out perfectly, but sometimes I stumble across a real winner. If no one ever risked making mistakes, we wouldn't have trailers, motor homes and fifth wheels to venture out in either!

Food without Salt

If you are used to sprinkling salt in everything you cook, and shaking it on everything you eat, the taste of food without it will take some getting used to, but it's not as bad as you may think. There are available commercial salt substitutes, which I personally can't stand. Perhaps you'll like them; some people do. Instead, I use a variety of spices and herbs to make dishes taste better. Garlic powder, onion powder, ground black or white pepper, ground ginger, and ground chili peppers are some of the spices I use. Try them in small quantities. Parsley, sage, rosemary, thyme, tarragon, and basil are my favourite herbs for salt substitution, either separately or in combinations.

Herbs and Spices for Salt-Free Boiled or Poached Eggs

Season eggs with a mixture of half garlic powder and half tarragon. You may make other mixtures by using onion powder instead of garlic, and parsley or basil in place of the tarragon.

Omelettes or Scrambled Eggs

Stir fry a combination of chopped onion, minced garlic, sliced mushrooms, red and green peppers, celery, minced fresh parsley, and other fresh herbs in the pan first. Take them out and cook the eggs. Mix in the vegetables and/or herbs just before serving, or spread them on the omelette before you fold it.

About Fat

People have become very conscious of the fat they eat, both because of links with blood cholesterol levels, and because of excess weight. Saturated fats found in animal products, coconut oil, and palm oil are considered to be the least healthy for people with high blood cholesterol levels. Reducing your intake of animal fats involves finding replacements for butter and lard, and buying low fat meats such as well-trimmed steak, extra lean ground meat, chicken or turkey breasts with the skin removed, rabbit, and veal. Coconut oil and palm oil are rarely used in the kitchen, but are often present in bought baked goods such as cookies, cakes, muffins, etc. So, if you buy baked goods, check the label to see what kind of fat has been used. If you bake for yourself, use soft vegetable margarine, or unsaturated oils such as safflower or canola oil. Another place to watch for saturated fats is in salad dressings. Again, when you make your own, you know for sure what's in it! If you like fried foods and need to watch your fat consumption, there are two good suggestions. Many people use cooking spray to keep the food from sticking. If you use a non-stick pan, or a cast iron pan that has been well-seasoned, you may not need cooking spray or fat.

Sugar

It's always the folks with the sweet tooth who end up with sugar problems, it seems! However, there are lots of products with artificial sweeteners on the market for them though. Traditionally, sugar is used not just to sweeten, but to enhance texture in a lot of foods. It's hard to change the habits of a lifetime but, if you can move to fresh fruit, raisins, nuts, and coconut to satisfy your longing for sweetness, these will all help fill the gap created by removing refined sugar from your menus.

Recipes

Here are some recipes I have developed using no added fat, salt, or sugar. Perhaps they will stimulate you to think of other ways to vary your menus while staying within your dietary restrictions. There are also recipes in the main part of the book that have less than the traditional amount of fat, salt, and sugar.

No-Fat, No-Salt, No-Sugar Potato Salad

This is a seriously healthy way to make potato salad, which you may have thought would be impossible to eat if you've restricted fat or salt or sugar in your diet. I cook double quantities of potatoes when I'm boiling them for supper, to make sure I have some on hand for this salad the next day.

1/2 cup	**nonfat yogurt**	**125 mL**
1 tsp	**dried basil**	**5 mL**
1/2 tsp	**dried crushed rosemary**	**2 mL**
1/2 tsp	**dried oregano**	**2 mL**
1/4 tsp	**ground black pepper**	**1 mL**
2 cups	**boiled potatoes**	**500 mL**
1	**stalk of celery, diced**	**1**

Mix the yogurt, herbs, and pepper together in a bowl and let stand to marry the flavours. If you're not restricted to no salt foods, you may add a pinch of salt. Cut the potatoes into small cubes and mix with the celery in a salad bowl. Pour the dressing over the vegetables, mix well and serve. Serves two.

Apple Salad - No Salt, No Sugar, Low Fat

This salad is based on a Waldorf salad that my mother used to make when I was small. The only fat in it is from the walnuts, so if you're really being purist about fat you may leave them out. I always thought it was quite outrageous of my mother to put nuts in a salad, and raisins too! Hers was mostly cabbage, but I prefer it this way, with none.

3	**apples, cored and chopped**	**3**
1/4	**onion, chopped**	**1/4**
1	**stalk celery, chopped**	**1**
1/4 cup	**raisins**	**50 mL**
1/4 cup	**walnut pieces**	**50 mL**
1/4 cup	**nonfat yogurt**	**50 mL**

Put the apples, onion, celery, raisins, and walnut pieces in a bowl. Pour the yogurt over it and mix well. Cover and chill in the refrigerator for half an hour or more before serving. Serves three or four. You can keep this in the refrigerator until the next day, if you don't eat it all in one sitting.

Curry and Walnut Dip/Dressing

1/2 cup	**nonfat yogurt**	**125 mL**
1 tbsp	**curry powder**	**15 mL**
1/4 cup	**chopped walnuts**	**50 mL**

Mix together and serve! If you want it sweeter, add a handful of raisins.

Delta Chicken BBQ

This is an alternative marinade for chicken breast strips (or veal) to be barbecued. If you cut the chicken in strips to start with, they will marinate faster, and two chicken breasts will serve three people. I made this up sitting by my friend Bonnie's house in Delta, BC, waiting for her to come home from work so we could have a visit. The neighbour exercised his horse in the paddock behind us. Across the road, a blueberry plantation was in bloom, and Canada geese strolled and pecked on the ploughed field next door. It's hard to believe that we were only twenty miles or so from downtown Vancouver.

BBQ Chicken Breast Strips

	juice of half a lemon	
	or	
2 tbsp	**bottled lemon juice**	**25 mL**
2 tsp	**Dijon mustard**	**10 mL**
1/2 tsp	**tarragon**	**2 mL**
1/2 tsp	**black pepper**	**2 mL**
2	**chicken breasts**	**2**
1 tsp	**sesame oil or vegetable oil for wiping the grill if needed**	**5 mL**
3	**hamburger buns**	**3**
	tomato slices	
	lettuce	
	mustard for spreading	
	sliced dill pickles	

In a bowl, combine the lemon juice, mustard, tarragon, and pepper. Trim any fat from the chicken breasts and cut them into half-inch strips. Put the chicken in the bowl, and mix well to cover it completely. Let it sit for at least an hour.

Preheat the barbecue. Then turn it down to low. Wipe the grill with oil to keep the chicken from sticking. Lay the strips of chicken on the grill. Cook with the lid closed. Use tongs to turn the chicken strips. They will only take a few minutes on each side. Toast the buns. Arrange the chicken strips on the buns and garnish with tomato slices, lettuce, mustard, and pickles. Serves three.

Minted Strawberries with Yogurt - No Added Fat or Sugar

It's very hot in southern California, even in the middle of April. The rattlesnakes come out to sun themselves, and the birds are busy nesting. The cactus flowers bloom, red, yellow, orange, and purple. All those wonderful fruits and vegetables that are imported to Canada are grown locally here. The strawberries are huge and delicious, just as they will be in Quebec in late June! Everyone slows down in the heat; those who live here have their ways of dealing with it. Certainly heating up the RV by cooking on the stove is a foolish thing to do. Here is a light dessert, no cooking required!

2 cups	**strawberries**	**500 mL**
1 cup	**nonfat plain yogurt**	**250 mL**
1/4 tsp	**dried crushed mint**	**1 mL**
	or	
2 tsp	**fresh chopped mint**	**10 mL**

Wash, hull, and slice the berries and divide them in two bowls. Spoon the yogurt on top and sprinkle on the mint. It's delicious, even without added sugar. Serves two.

The Journey
Continues

I am writing this sitting in a picnic area near Canmore, Alberta, gazing at snow-capped mountains on a bright sunny June afternoon. There's a gopher popping his (or her) head up from time to time to stare at the motor home. A couple parked and walked along beside the railway line. They spoke to Alex, who is up on the roof installing our solar panels, on their way back to their truck. They didn't ask him where we're from or where we're going. Just as well. Our license plate shows British Columbia now, and that's where we get our mail, but we haven't been there enough to feel we really come from there. Where are we going next? Well, we're planning to attend a rally in Medicine Hat next weekend, but, other than that, we really don't know, and it's fine.

The past ten months of living on the road have been great. We used to drive fifty thousand miles a year between the two of us, going back and forth to work and taking trips here and there. Now we're averaging two thousand miles a month, together, and we see a whole lot more.

Each day brings a new adventure. We walked up the trail to the Grassi Lakes early this morning, and watched the clouds lift off the mountain peaks. I saw a moose last week, kneeling to drink from a pool by the side of the road. He rose to his feet and stared as I drove past. Alex met some very friendly helpful folks at the welding shop in Longview a few days ago, who straightened out our bumper and welded it back on. I strolled along a fence line and noticed one gopher, a white cabbage butterfly, and four different kinds of yellow wildflowers. One was a dandelion, but I don't know the names of the others. For now, this gypsy life suits us very well. People all over the country are friendly, curious about what we're up to, and generally happy with their lives. The land is beautiful. Flowers bloom. Trees sprout fresh green leaves and needles. Birds sing madly in the morning, and deer vault gracefully over a fence.

Cooking has long been a special joy for me. The act of creating wholesome, delicious, simple meals for myself and the folks I'm most fond of is a great source of satisfaction to me. I hope you enjoy these recipes and stories as much as I have!

I'm always looking for more recipes that are delicious, nutritious, pleasing to the eye, and simple to prepare. If you have any suggestions, comments or stories you'd like to share, do write to me, care of the publisher. Perhaps one day we'll meet down the road and swap stories at Happy Hour with glasses of fresh lemonade and snacks.

Index

For more copies of

A Taste For Travel: The R.V. Cookbook

send $10.95 plus $3.00 for GST, shipping and handling to:

GENERAL STORE PUBLISHING HOUSE
1 Main Street, Burnstown, Ontario
Canada, K0J 1G0
(613) 432-7697 or 1-800-465-6072
Fax (613) 432-7184
e-mail: genstorpublish@renc.igs.net

The Triple E Story

Customer Satisfaction the Key to Triple E's Success

Excellence and Elegance through Engineering – this underlying philosophy is the cornerstone to the success of Canada's largest recreational vehicle manufacturer, Triple E Recreational Vehicles (a division of Triple E Canada Ltd.) This is Triple E's 31st year of production which included a variety of recreational vehicles for a global marketplace. With the continual challenge of meeting the needs of its customers Triple E is in a position that would have been hard to imagine when the company began more than three decades ago.

In 1965, P.W. Enns, who owned a plumbing and heating business in Winkler, Manitoba, took an interest in travel trailers while on a voluntary missions assignment in Elkhart, Indiana. Being an inquisitive person who enjoyed trying new things, Enns bought a torsion axle and brought it home to Winkler. Enlisting the aid of his two sons-in-law, Philipp Ens and Peter Elias, the three men set out to build the first Triple E trailer, a 13-foot, aerodynamic design they called the Compact. Sales amounted to 50 pieces the first year, 97 the next and 327 in 1967. With the success of the first design, they also added a 16-foot model in 1967 giving families an affordable way to visit Montreal's Expo.

The company's facilities have grown from 5,000 sq. ft. to over 200,000 sq. ft., and personnel from 10 to 200. In 1969, Triple E was sold to Jim Pattison, who was then acquiring many Canadian recreational vehicle manufacturers. This was a welcomed transition as Mr. Pattison brought with him the needed expertise and marketing skills to support the rapid expansion of Triple E. The three E's remained with the company and continued to develop new products. The oil embargo of 1973 hit the motoring industries hard, causing Pattison to sell the company back to Philipp Ens and P.W. Enns, who has since retired from the business.

There have been setbacks over the years but Triple E has always reacted in a way that allowed them to recover positively. One of these setbacks was a fire in 1972 that destroyed the entire manufacturing facility. The company bounced right back by purchasing the business and facilities of another manufacturer in Winkler. They moved right in and continued production in short order. Today the recreational vehicle division complex operation includes the main assembly plant, welding and fibreglass fabrication, painting facilities, wood mill, customer service, and general office.

For the first 24 years of production, sales were exclusively in Canada. In 1988, the company expanded sales into the European market, starting with the Scandinavian countries which at that time accounted for 10% of production. Soon thereafter Germany was added and this opened the door to other markets including Japan.

Triple E's expansion into the United States was a direct result of the Canadian product meeting the high quality and winterization demands of customers stretching south of the border. The company continues to build a network of dealers throughout the U.S. market and currently has dealers from New York to Florida.

In 1980 Lode-King Industries of Winkler, Manitoba started to produce commercial highway trailers for the trucking industry. Lode-King products are marketed throughout Canada.

In 1989 Mr. P.W. Enns decided to step down as Chairman of the Board and Mr. Philipp R. Ens, the President and General Manager, was appointed to the position. In 1993 Mr. Ens appointed Mr. Terry Elias, the son of Peter Elias and grandson of P.W. Enns, as General Manager and Chief Operating Officer of the company. In 1996 Mr. Elias was appointed President of Triple E Canada, and continues to direct the day-to-day operation of all Triple E companies.

Mr. Phil Ens suggests that the reason Triple E has remained competitive in today's recreational industry is due to their philosophy. Build the product the customer wants and build it competitively. It's that simple! Winkler is a predominantly Mennonite community and the people here have a tremendous work ethic. Our products are well designed and constructed. Our commitment to customer satisfaction remains our primary concern and we all continue to listen to our customers to improve the product.

In spite of the challenges from time to time which include the fire, the slow downs, the recessions, Triple E Recreational Vehicles remains firm in their belief that they will continue to produce quality products. We will meet the expectations of our customers and provide employment for the people of the local and surrounding communities of Winkler. Our commitment to our staff, suppliers, customers and community will allow us to maintain the reputation of integrity and quality for the future.